MW00570895

1,000,000 Books

are available to read at

www.ForgottenBooks.com

Read online
Download PDF
Purchase in print

ISBN 978-1-332-23878-1
PIBN 10302741

This book is a reproduction of an important historical work. Forgotten Books uses
state-of-the-art technology to digitally reconstruct the work, preserving the original format
whilst repairing imperfections present in the aged copy. In rare cases, an imperfection in
the original, such as a blemish or missing page, may be replicated in our edition. We do,
however, repair the vast majority of imperfections successfully; any imperfections that
remain are intentionally left to preserve the state of such historical works.

Forgotten Books is a registered trademark of FB &c Ltd.
Copyright © 2018 FB &c Ltd.
FB &c Ltd, Dalton House, 60 Windsor Avenue, London, SW19 2RR.
Company number 08720141. Registered in England and Wales.

For support please visit www.forgottenbooks.com

1 MONTH OF
FREE
READING

at

www.ForgottenBooks.com

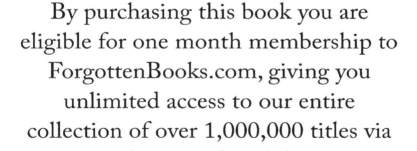

By purchasing this book you are eligible for one month membership to ForgottenBooks.com, giving you unlimited access to our entire collection of over 1,000,000 titles via our web site and mobile apps.

To claim your free month visit:

www.forgottenbooks.com/free302741

* Offer is valid for 45 days from date of purchase. Terms and conditions apply.

English
Français
Deutsche
Italiano
Español
Português

www.forgottenbooks.com

Mythology Photography **Fiction**
Fishing Christianity **Art** Cooking
Essays Buddhism Freemasonry
Medicine **Biology** Music **Ancient
Egypt** Evolution Carpentry Physics
Dance Geology **Mathematics** Fitness
Shakespeare **Folklore** Yoga Marketing
Confidence Immortality Biographies
Poetry **Psychology** Witchcraft
Electronics Chemistry History **Law**
Accounting **Philosophy** Anthropology
Alchemy Drama Quantum Mechanics
Atheism Sexual Health **Ancient History**
Entrepreneurship Languages Sport
Paleontology Needlework Islam
Metaphysics Investment Archaeology
Parenting Statistics Criminology
Motivational

UNIV. OF
CALIFORNIA

Forestry Library

Michigan's Millions of Idle Acres

Written by

P. S. LOVEJOY,

Of the University of Michigan Forestry Faculty;

and

FRED E. JANETTE,

Of The Detroit News Staff.

A Series of Articles Published in The Detroit News, May 24-June 4.

Published by The Detroit News, June, 1920.

UNIV. OF
CALIFORNIA

Agric.-Forestry. Main Libra·

While the world suffers from a shortage of forest products, millions of acres of Michigan land that once yielded vast wealth in timber are today waste lands, fire-swept and deteriorating year by year. Forward-looking men who are wrestling with the problem believe that the people of Michigan do not realize the gravity of the situation or the possibility of remedy. Their plan is to restore to the wasted areas of this state the forest industry.

The series of articles to follow will present a study of the causes and conditions creating Michigan's waste areas in the northern part of the state, and give an account of what is being done to restore them to use.

P. S. Lovejoy, who contributes the first article of the series, is a member of the University of Michigan forestry faculty, a scientist and a practical woodsman of long experience.

By P. S. LOVEJOY
Of the Forestry Faculty, University of Michigan.

A third of Michigan virtually is bankrupt, unable to pay its way with schools and roads, getting poorer instead of richer from year to year, producing less and less of value.

This third of Michigan takes 10,000,000 acres or so, the most of it being in the northern part of the Lower Peninsula, the rest in the Upper Peninsula.

The bulk of these bankrupt lands were originally in pine forest. From 1870 to 1900 Michigan led the world in the quantity, quality and value of its timber exports. Today Michigan is a tremendous importer of timber and other forest products. This is unusual but not in itself a proof that anything is radically wrong. Ohio, also, was covered originally with timber and is now a great timber importer, and is, nevertheless, prosperous and thriving.

LAND GOES TO DISUSE.

But in the case of Ohio, the removal of the forests was followed promptly by intensive agricultural development; the land went from a lower to a higher kind of use. In Michigan the removal of the original forests has not been followed by any other profitable use of the land save on about two-thirds of the state, the balance of the land, being today non-productive and "waste." The bulk of these idle lands has been deserted and has been non-productive for upward of 20 years and there is no accident about it. Most of the idle lands are sandy and poor. As a rule, pine follows the sands as willows follow the creeks.

If Iowa were to be forced to import corn from New York or if California sent to Florida for oranges, it would be no more preposterous than to have Michigan, with 10,000,000 acres of idle stump land, importing great quantities of forest products. We do that.

Michigan-grown hemlock, shipped 200 miles, sells at the same price in Detroit as does fir grown on the Pacific Coast and shipped 2,000 miles. The hickory for the wheels of Michigan automobiles is coming from Arkansas and Mississippi. The oak for Grand Rapids furniture is being cut in Louisiana and Tennessee. Michigan does not even supply itself with enough telephone poles and railroad ties, but imports poles from Idaho and ties from Virginia.

—3—

450960

TIMBER-EXPORTS GROW.

Much of the paper on which our newspapers are being printed is made from Canadian spruce. Box-boards are being shipped in from Pennsylvania and Arkansas and California. The state imports much more timber than it cuts and cuts much more timber than it grows, constantly grows and cuts less and constantly imports more.

The freight bill on imported lumber alone is costing Michigan around $2,000,000 a year, and each year the freight bill is due to increase greatly as the sources of supply recede with the steady devastation of the forests of the South and West. Meanwhile Michigan continues to support 10,000,000 acres or so of idle lands which a few years ago were producing the most generally useful kinds of timber the world ever had. White pine lumber practically is out of the market. There is not a town of 5,000 in the state which does not import yellow pine from the Gulf states.

On the face of things, such economic arrangements do not appear very reasonable, but they are easy to account for. If we could get the timber we needed from the neighbors, and at easy prices, why bother with growing timber and why fuss about the situation?

SUPPLY DECREASES.

Perhaps that might be an all right way of doing save for one item— the neighbor's supply of timber is not holding out.

Withing the lifetime of many persons now living, the center of the lumber industry has moved from the New England country to Pennsylvania, to the Lake states, to the Gulf states. The Southern Pine Association reports that within 10 years 3,000 big sawmills will be junked and cut out and gone, and that the cut of Southern pine must drop about 50 per cent. That leaves us the virgin forests of the Pacific Coast. The United States Bureau of Corporations recently made a very elaborate check on the timber left in the United States and gives us 60 years to use up all the log timber at the present rates of consumption. That's only long enough to grow a really nice set of whiskers. Already the Pacific Coast timber, with a two or three thousand-mile haul, is to be found in all the larger towns of the East. So the lumber industry has made its last jump.

HERE IS CHOICE.

When the Coast timber begins to run short, in 20 years or so, we can take our pick between Russian timber and Amazon timber, or we can do without timber. If we do not care for those alternatives, of course we can grow some more timber, and pulp wood, and cooperage and box stuff, and trees to yield turpentine and rosin and tannic acid and acetic acid and wood alcohol and charcoal and rifle butts and airplane propellers and lead pencils and clothes pins and ax handles and bridge timbers and railroad ties and such other items as seem useful to have around in generous quantities, when and where needed, and which come from the forests and from no place else.

Whenever we get ready we can grow all the timber we want. Growing timber is a simple affair. All you have to do is to stick a little tree into the right sort of ground and wait.

PROCESS OF PLANTING.

If you want pine or spruce trees, and if you do not want to depend on luck, first you get the fresh cones from the trees and take out the seed. Then you put the seed where it will be happy and in a couple of years you have a pine or spruce tree as long as your little finger. Then you pick out the ground to set-it in, and that is easier than with some other plants. You can't look at a field and tell just how good a place it is for buckwheat or timothy, but if you have a piece of land covered with big old pine and spruce stumps, you dont' have to be a soil chemist to find out whether pine or spruce will grow again where they have once done well.

But one does not like to use rose ground for sunflowers or corn ground for buckwheat. Each crop belongs in its place. We could raise a lot of very fine cottonwood in the corn belt country, but we never will. Each crop should go into its appointed place. If we want to raise timber we ought to find out where it can be grown to the best advantage, everything considered. That is a very simple matter.

MANY ACRES OF "WASTE."

Michigan, for instance, has something over 10,000,000 acres of idle land which once grew fine pine, but which is now idle land. Wisconsin and Minnesota have twice as much of that land as has Michigan. Georgia has 20,000,000 acres, and a dozen other states have from 5,000,000 to 15,000,000 acres each of idle, cut-over, logged-off, non-productive, "waste" land.

As a matter of fact, we have so much idle former forest land that it has become embarrassing. Germany is bigger than France, and Texas is bigger than Germany. If you blocked up the cut-over forest lands of the United States and put them down over Texas, they would cover that sizable state and thousands of square miles would stick out over the edges. If you wanted to survey those cut-over lands and cross each square mile once, and had an airplane, and made 100 miles an hour, and traveled 10 hours a day, your trip would take you the greater part of a year.

TIME IS A FACTOR.

So there isn't any difficulty about finding a suitable place to grow timber if ever we decide we want to do such a thing. Whenever we get ready we can get the seed and the ground is waiting, and that is all there is to it except the matter of time which is required between planting and harvest. A tree takes its own time about growing, and no amount of urgency or money can hurry it up very much. But we know how fast the different species grow under different conditions, and we know how long we will have to wait in order to harvest pulp wood or ax handles or bridge timbers. The average tree from which our common lumber is coming is around 250 years old. Most of our paper is made from spruce, and the average spruce cut for pulp is over 100 years old. But, by matching the right species to the right soil, and helping out here and there, we know how to get a right decent sawlog in 100 years or even less, and we know how to grow a very satisfactory kind of pulp wood in less than 50 years.

TIME TO START FORESTS.

Considering all these things, it would seem that the only important thing left was to determine whether we wanted to begin raising timber as a crop, and if so, just when. And if the Bureau of Corporations is right in saying that our old virgin sawlog timber will be gone at the present rate of consumption in 60 years, and if it is true that the pulp mills are so short of spruce that they are moving into Canada, and if it is true that the Canadian authorities report that they are finding out that they have very much less spruce than they thought, and if it takes at least 100 years to make sawlogs and some 50 years to make good pulp wood, it might seem advisable to do a little something in the way of starting new forests in the fairly near future, as it were. But one should go rather slow with radical innovations, of course, and look before he leaps and not do anything foolish and not get run off his feet by sentimental considerations, and be calm and take it easy and rather look out for log-haired theorists—and that is just what we have been doing.

PINE NEARLY OFF MARKET.

While we have been taking it easy the undisputed fact has developed that hemlock lumber costs around $60 a thousand feet in Michigan and that white pine is practically off the market; that Michigan has more than 10,000,000 acres of idle former forest land and a constantly growing freight bill on imported lumber; that the pulp mills are moving to Canada; that we are the most generous users of forest products in the world; that France and Germany have for centuries kept about a fourth of their entire land area in productive forests and still have been forced to import more and more timber—and that, within 50 years, in spite of anything we can now do, we shall be down to a per capita consumption of timber no greater than that to which France and Germany have become adjusted through many centuries and with which they are barely able to maintain their industries.

Really, the only question is: Will it take hemlock lumber at $100 a thousand feet and news print at 10 cents a pound to get us started? Nothing now can prevent such prices except the starting of new forests which can come into maturity so as to fill the great timber deficit which will be evident enough within 50 years.

WARNING RIDICULED.

There is nothing at all new about all these things. Thirty-five years ago Dr. Spaulding, at the University of Michigan, had it figured out that it would be well to keep Michigan's pine lands at work. He was laughed at. Practical people, especially the lumbermen, informed him that there was "enough pine in Michigan to last forever"—and believed it, too. Twenty years ago Charles Garfield, of Grand Rapids, saw what was coming and tried to get something done, and was laughed at. Practical people, especially the lumbermen, stated that it was a well-known fact that "pine would not follow pine." Fifteen years ago Prof. Roth told the state officials that if they would let him run the tax-reverted state lands he would make them pay and could build them up into properties which would yield a fair rate of interest on a valuation of $50 an acre. For this he was called names and some of the newspapers had a lot of fun about it—print paper then being easy to get and not worth 4 cents a pound.

NOTHING BEING DONE.

So things have run along in the good old way and now we are caught short, and good old Michigan has a third of her acres out of a job and getting poorer, year by year. And still nobody is doing much of anything about it all. It's just as well to be practical, you know.

If you travel around the state and ask questions, the chances are that almost everybody you meet will agree that it would be a right good idea for somebody to start in growing some timber as a sort of regular crop. If you ask where it would be practicable to begin, probably you would be told that the Government was doing something or other out West. Weren't there national forests or something? Haven't we a state forest some place up-state? There are and we have. But of all the timber left in the United States less than 15 per cent is on the national forests, and of all the timber cut last year less than 3 per cent came from the national forests, the balance being from privately owned forests.

RAGGED LITTLE PATCHES.

And the state forests of Michigan consist of ragged little patches of country so thoroughly logged off and so burned over that the owners quit paying taxes on them. Altogether, the state forests aggregate a fraction of a million acres and the state has a full 10,000,000 acres of idle lands not in the state forests. So the existing Federal and state forests are not going to help very soon or very much.

If you inquire you will find that the bulk of the idle lands are owned by lumbermen or former lumbermen. If you look sharply you may discover that it is written into the Washington records that some 30-odd concerns "own" some 6,000,000 acres of Michigan—a sixth of the state. If you interview some of these concerns and ask how they managed to pick up so much land you will not be treated with courtesy. If you ask what they propose to do with so much land you will be told that it is none of your business. If you ask why they prefer idle and non-productive land to land covered with growing timber you will be sneered at and told about the fires. If you ask why they don't keep the fires out you will get an impatient answer to the effect that fire and idle brush land go together as do fleas and a dog—and that, anyway, it is up to the state to keep out the fires.

WHAT STATE SAYS.

If you ask about it at Lansing you will find out that the game warden is also the fire warden; that he reports to the Public Domain Commission, and that the Public Domain Commission feels very strongly that fires are quite a misfortune in the state. The secretary of the Public Domain Commission is also immigration commissioner, and, if you ask, he will give you some nicely illustrated literature concerning the wonderful agricultural possibilities of the cut-over country, concerning further details of which you are referred to the state geologist and the Agricultural College.

If you want to make a nuisance of yourself and travel further around the spiral the state geologist will tell you that he has nothing like a soil survey of the idle lands; that he would like to have and regrets that he has not and, therefore, that he can not, unfortunately, furnish the details concerning which you ask.

DETAILS ARE SCARCE.

Then you can try the Agricultural College and the folks there will also regret that no real soil survey has ever been made; that detailed information concerning the location, nature, value and possibilities of

—7—

the cut-over country is rather scant, and that they would be perfectly delighted if someone would get something done about it, and why not find out just what it was that happened to the Soil Survey Law which passed the Legislature a couple of years back?

Back at the State House you will be told that there was such an act, that it was passed by the Legislature and signed by the Governor, and then, as a measure of war economy, something happened which let the appropriation lapse, and why not ask about that at the Governor's office?

CASE OF BANKRUPTCY.

Put it in common business talk and it comes out clearer. What is the essential nature of the case? Why, it's a case of bankruptcy; some millions of acres of land do not pay enough in taxes to cover the cost of assessing and collecting the taxes and attending to the administrative routine. The owners and the interested parties do not seem to be able to fix things up. Creditors are getting uneasy. What's to be done in a case like that? Oh, get a receiver appointed.

All right, now we have a receiver. What will be do? The very first thing will be to stop the wasting of assets. Then he will 'have a full inventory made. Then, having found out just what he has on his hands, having located liabilities and assets, he can proceed to plan things so as to wind up the concern or get it on its feet again.

Our receiver will find that to stop the wasting of assets it a real job. The biggest item will be in getting rid of the fires. If it had not been for the fires all those idle acres would today be producing timber— good timber and lots of it; the lands would have stayed productive if it had not been for the fires.

CARELESSNESS IS CAUSE.

To keep fires out of a forest country is not easy, but still it is simple enough. First you must prevent them from getting started if possible. About 95 per cent of all fires are due to carelessness. To cure that sort of carelessness requires large doses of skillfully administered publicity—an advertising campaign. Also a little law enforcement. A little law enforcement would increase the publicity, too. Matter of novelty and surprise generates interest, as it were. A lot of the fires could be prevented from starting.

But some fires will start in spite of all one could do. The job of putting them out is simple enough. The first thing is to have a system of lookouts and patrolmen which can detect the presence of a fire within a few minutes of its start, get its exact location, and report the facts to headquarters. Headquarters then sizes up the situation and sends a competent crew equipped adequately so as to get it to the site of the fire within an hour or so after the fire first showed up. The crew then puts out the fire, or if it can't, that fact is reported back swiftly and reinforcements come in a-flying.

WHAT ABOUT COST?

If the receiver for the bankrupt part of Michigan has all this explained to him he will begin to be doubtful. "All very well," he will say, "but what about the cost of all those roads and trails and lookouts and telephone lines and tools and what-not? How could I ever justify such expenses?"

"By preventing the wasting of assets," he will be told. "It's costing you a whole lot more right now, in losses, than it would to prevent those losses. Sooner or later, every acre of all that idle country is going to be put to profitable work. It will be made to grow something. Maybe farm crops, maybe forage crops, maybe timber crops, but all of them depending on the soil. The better the soil the better the crops —and the other way around, too. Now fire destroys the organic matter in the soil, and that means the humus and the nitrogen. Nitrogen is already the limiting factor in most of our soils. And a common every-summer fire running over fresh-cut forest or virgin forest, will burn up organic material containing nitrogen that would cost you, on the market, around a hundred dollars and up. Every succeeding fire takes a little more and, finally, just about every bit of it.

FERTILITY BURNED OUT.

"That's the biggest reason these lands are idle and why so many millions of acres are worthless for farming. Fertility has been burned out. To prevent that will be worth vastly more than the cost of stopping fires.

"Or you could justify it another way. Figure the cost of replacing the young trees burned up. Take the extra low costs of raising and planting trees on the State Forests and apply that to the number of good young trees that burn and it runs into millions of dollars every year or so. The fires have killed out most of the pines and other good trees, but they keep trying to get back and, with half a chance, a lot of the country would go back into pulp and log timber in just a few years. To prevent fire losses in young timber would justify the cost of stopping fire.

"Or figure it out on another basis. What is the north country worth for recreation purposes? How much money do people spend in order to get into a cool and pleasant green land where there is good fishing and hunting and a fine place to play?

FIGURE TOURIST BILL.

"Add up the money spent for railroad fares and automobile traffic and in hotel bills and in building and maintaining summer homes, and the business developed for summer tourist traffic and from hunting and fishing and trapping, and what's the gross? If it were so low as $15,000,000 a year, that would be about a dollar an acre for all the idle land and the good land in the north part of the state. But 'how much tourist and summer traffic will develop in a country full of black stumps and scraggy brush and smoke, where one never knows when it is safe to take a side road or when his camp may be burned out or how often fire will burn over his favorite hunting and fishing grounds? To stop the fires would be a good investment on this count alone.'

"Well, that sounds all right," the receiver might say, "but what would it cost to stop the fires?"

The answer to that would be that 5 cents an acre a year would do it if it were properly spent. If that runs up into a lot more money than has been spent for fire-fighting in the past it is because, while we have had some fire-fighting, we have never had fire protection.

MIGHT GET OLD ACT.

If the receiver we have supposed to be appointed for the bankrupt area of Michigan were a long-headed receiver, after checking things over a while, probably he would decide: "It would be worth it, but we could never put it over without more backing than we could expect to get—unless .. Wonder if the newspaper could be made to see this?"

Suppose the price of newsprint went on up to five cents and then seven cents a pound and the newspapers did see it and the fire job was really taken hold of and was working out, the receiver's next job would be to get an inventory of his layout. Maybe he could get again into life the old act that passed the Legislature and received the Governor's signature and then died. Then there would be crews out in the brush, running lines, taking soil samples, mapping the old timber and the young timber and the brush areas and the farm and grazing lands and generally taking stock of what there is in the shop. •

GOOD FARMING LAND.

When the reports came in and were worked up, the receiver could open a tract-book and say: "There's 9,000 acres of really good land which, right now, as things are, could be farmed profitably. Ought to be farmed. Jake, look up this tract and find out why it isn't being farmed and dope me out a good scheme of getting the right folks on that land right away."

Or it might be grazing land which, as things are right now, is undoubtedly capable of supporting a profitable grazing development. The receiver could proceed to get that unit to work.

When a lot of the really first-class tracts were being settled there would be time to figure out what to do with the balance of the propery. Some of it would, obviously, be worth more for growing timber than for anything else. The land classification would indicate just where such lands were located and just what condition they were in. The receiver could turn such lands over to somebody who understood that sort of work.

INVENTORY COMPLETE.

Finally, there would be left a lot of land of dubious character; not of a quality or area or location to permit a profitable agricultural or profitable grazing development now, as things actually are, and still, perhaps or probably, useful for such purposes in the future. Maybe some land would need drainage, other land might be all right, but too expensive to clear, other land just beyond the edge of profitable use in agriculture because of soil conditions.

With those lands the receiver could take his time, being very busy putting real settlers on real farm lands and real timber on real timber lands. He could take his time about the balance of the lands of dubious character. He might find ways of working them into use or he might let them lie idle, or he might turn them into timber producers pending the time they might become more useful for something else. Anyway, having his inventory, he would know what he had, the condition it was in and what he would have to do to get all his property to work.

STEPS TOWARD INVENTORY.

All of which is a nice little picture but nothing but "dope."

And that is the way things stacked up until this spring. In April there was a meeting of the Michigan Academy of Science and a special session devoted to the discussion of these affairs. The resolutions finally adopted called for the reinstatement of the soil and economy survey of appropriation and an amendment of the original law so as to provide an expert Board of Control to advise with the State Geologist as to the best ways of running such a survey. So far so good; steps have been taken looking toward a real inventory of our state's lands.

But to complete such a job properly will take years and years, and in the meantime settlers are settling, assessors are assessing, tourists are touring, fires are burning, forests are disappearing and a third of the state loafs in desolation. There are those, perhaps, who, hesitating over the prospects, may recommend that nothing be done until the big inventory job is all complete. A good excuse for doing nothing can always find a welcome home, but not that excuse for this occasion.

MAPS TO BE AVAILABLE.

It was reported at the Academy of Science meeting that a set of maps was already in existence, which, with a little editing, would serve excellently as a stop-gap between the almost total lack of information under which we now labor, and the final completion of the big-job inventory. Those maps will shortly be made available, no doubt.

According to the Academy of Science, the most urgent step in any program calculated to put all the state's acres to permanent and profitable work is the stopping of the fires. This can be done: is perfectly practicable, said the Academy. This is the job of the Public Domain Commission, and it is up to the Commission to get after the job in the very near future, said the Academy. All of which is 'just more "dope," perhaps.

BIG TREE NURSERY.

To be sure, the forest rangers on the National Forests are catching fires while they are little, and putting up their lookouts and telephone lines and working their heliographs and caching their fire-tools along the trails and making arrests when somebody gets inexcusably careless with fire in the woods, and, of course, up at the State Forest near Grayling, the state forester is putting tractor-plowed fire lines about his plantations, and keeping out the fire in spite of the fact that the counry all around him burns over every little while. And, of course, he is running one of the biggest forest tree nurseries in the world and planting millions of little pines on the poor old lumbered-over, burned-off, tax-reverted "waste" lands of the state, and making them grow right along as nicely as can be. even though the lumberman knew that "pine would not follow pine."

And, to be sure, the secretary of one of the development associations says that "Wisconsin is getting ten good settlers to Michigan's one. Wisconsin has a real soil survey and acts as though she wanted to get settlers, whereas Michigan—but what's the use?"

PLAYING IT SAFE.

Seeing that things are as they are, and that we are practical people, not visionary; with our feet on the ground; progressive, to be sure, but not carried away by theories and radical notions; playing it safe and sound, rather than fussing about the hypothetical future, the mere fact that a third of Michigan, 10,000,000 acres or so, is idle, barren, fire-spent, getting poorer and more desolate, is nothing of any particular importance. Hemlock lumber is only $60 a thousand and newsprint only 4 cents a pound. If, for any reason, the future should bring hemlock to $100 a thousand and newsprint to 10 cents per pound, why, then, if it seems an appropriate thing to do, the matter may receive adequate attention. Or it may not. Timber is a long-time crop and no degree of urgency and no amount of money can hurry it to maturity.

(In the article leading this series, devoted to a study of Michigan's waste land problem and a project for making the disused areas once more productive, P. S. Lovejoy of the University of Michigan Forestry faculty, stated that "a third of Michigan virtually is bankrupt," told of the wealth in forest products that this area once produced, and outlined a program of restoration. He covered a vast geographical area and a far-reaching economic problem in a condensed statement. The Detroit News has undertaken to explain the details from sources of information arising on the land itself, and to try to make clear what is being done to cope with the problem, what might be done, what the benefits would be to the whole State and to users of forest products—which is everybody everywhere—and how the individual citizen of Michigan can help. The following ten articles are devoted to that purpose.)

By FRED E. JANETTE.
(of The Detroit News Staff)

ARTICLE I.

Two errors of judgment, not unnatural to their day and generation, the same misjudgment that operated to produce bankrupt lands in many sections of the country, worked in the minds of Michigan citizens in the palmy days of the lumber industry. These errors of judgment were, first, that there was so much forest that the supply of lumber and other forest products was practically inexhaustible; and, second, that farms would follow and keep relative pace with forest clearing.

Everybody now sees and feels the effects of these mistakes. On the one hand we have a lumber shortage which means costs of dizzy height —lumber in general has advanced 97 per cent in price in the last 12 months—and on the other hand we have, here in Michigan alone, 3,000,000 acres of one-time forest land in arrears for taxes; a record of more than 2,300,000 acres in arrears for 5 years running, reverted to the state, literally bankrupt and foreclosed; with millions more so unproductive that they have to lean on wealthier sections of the state for support for their roads and schools and other public necessities. And there are 5,000,000 acres on the tax rolls of an assessed valuation of $5 an acre, average; the taxes not collectable on vast stretches of them.

SECOND OF ERRORS.

This is the picture in plain black and white, and merely outlined, of a non-productive and sometimes absolutely bankrupt area three times as large as the whole state of Connecticut.

There are 36,000,000 land acres within Michigan. In round numbers, sufficient for comparative purposes, 18,000,000 are in farms. Now one comes to consideration of the second of the primal errors of Michigan's citizenry in the palmy days of the lumber industry—that "farms would follow the lumberman." They actually thought that the denudation of the land in those days, with no replacement of the forest wealth, was a blessing—that the forest was a foe that had to be conquered to give the agriculturist his chance. There is a remnant of that tradition still to be found lurking in the remoter sections of northern Michigan. But it has finally sifted down, in the main, to the minds of that species of gentry with which the state is all too familiar—the sort engaged in selling lands of starvation quality to ignorant home seekers. The lumber industry is pretty well gone, or going, in upper Michigan, but the "sucker" industry is still going, with growing handicaps.

—12—

HAS NOT KEPT PACE.

The total farm area in this state, exclusive of the fruit farms, is 8,856,000 acres. That is part of the area which the statisticians allot out of the state's 36,000,000 acres to the farmer. It is the part which the agriculturist has actually improved. Then there is an allotment of 6,000,000 more acres—conceded, proclaimed and properly advertised as farm land of sufficient worth to pay a living if worked. But it has not been improved. Without setting foot on the millions of bankrupt acres with view to tillage. the farmer has a field within the confines of this state as big as the State of New Hampshire in which he has not even broken ground.

This tells two stories in one breath. It tells how agriculture has NOT kept pace with land clearing; and it tells how unmitigatedly foolish, when not actually criminal, is the "sucker" industry of selling thin sand lands in remote Michigan to men who might be working on better land.

NOT ALL BANKRUPT.

But if we are going to get anywhere that will be a departure point for going forward we must be fair. Perhaps the passing use of the term North Michigan in the foregoing is not understood as meant. The bankrupt lands of Michigan are in Northern Michigan. But not all North Michigan lands are bankrupt lands, nor even starvation farming lands. Right here this newspaper takes pleasure in falling back upon its own record in this matter. Many columns have been printed in recent years to make known the successful efforts of agriculturists on northern lands and to hearten the state with prophecy of wealth in foodstuffs that bade fair to come from them. Not a word of all this is now recanted. The lands were there then, and they are there now—the most of them awaiting the exact discovery that waits on a land inventory. But if the lands are there and farms are there, the farmers are not in any such numbers as of old The explanation does not need to be made at length. It is high wages in the towns and cities. Nevertheless, these lands are agricultural lands, and not waste lands, not in the category of the 10,000,000 virtually bankrupt lands. They are oases in a desert.

Our business in the former days was. on the oases Now we are about to explore and appraise the desert, leaving the farmer to raise farm crops and see who can raise a crop on the desert, and what. Just one thing is insisted on: while "one man is trying to work 160 acres in the best sections of the state," which Dean Shaw, of the Michigan Agricultural College, has told the writer is a common fact, and while there are approximately 1,750,000 idle farm acres in Michigan because there are not farmers enough, it will continue to be insisted and taken for granted that attempt to divert farmers on to lands that haven't been able to pay taxes for a period of years is economic criminality and ought to stop—especially as there is a better way to restore the desert to production.

INQUIRE INTO OWNERSHIP.

Dropping the term "desert," which doesn't sound nice, let the inquiry be into the ownership and present control as a property of the bankrupt empire of 10,000,000 acres. The end in view is an answer to the question, how best to make these unused acres productive. The land, its amount, location and control are the first consideration.; then the care of what of value may now exist on the land; lastly, improvement by cultural methods.

The areas considered in connection with this inquiry as to the possibility of restoring the forests are located, some areas small, some large in all the northern counties above a line drawn from Saginaw Bay to Lake Michigan, taking in, as the southern tier of counties in the area to be examined, Arenac, Gladwin, Clare, Osceola, Lake and Mason. This means all north Michigan, including the upper peninsula—42 counties. Just as there are some of the best lands in the state north of this line, notably in the Upper Peninsula, there are bankrupt lands below it. But the area defined is logically to be called the area wherein lies the bankrupt lands of Michigan.

REVERTING TO STATE.

Corporations and individuals own by far the largest number of acres, and their holdings include vast areas of non-productive lands. These are the cut-over timber lands, memento of the by-gone lumber industry, standing idle, fire-swept from year to year, on the books, of course, as an asset—as a matter of fact when the interests of the whole state and all its people are considered, a liability. Among these private holdings are millions of acres verging from those on the assessors' books at $5 an acre or less to the ones which the owners are allowing to revert to the state because of non-payment of taxes. What private persons own, exactly, as to the number of acres, is not so important except from this last consideration—as a reservoir from which flows a continuous stream of acreage into the state's ownership. It is with state ownership that the present problem has to do, as of first consideration. It is the land to which they themselves hold title that the people of Michigan can regard as the first element in the problem of what to do to make the idle acres again grow trees. What private persons do or won't do can be forgotten for the time being. The state has its own land, idle, non-productive, and public attention can with most profit be turned in that direction.

The public owned lands are of several sorts. State tax lands are of largest volume. There are University and Agricultural College lands, and Federal areas of comparatively small size. It is the state tax lands at which, and to the administration of which, the people of Michigan must look for practical experimentation in the labor of restoring the idle lands to profitable use.

SOME IS RESOLD.

When private owners have failed to pay taxes for five years the land involved may by law be deemed abandoned. and it becomes state property. The Auditor-General gets it. He has thus acquired, for the people of the state, 2,300,000 acres since 1893. The reversion of this "five-year" land to the state is continuous, reversions occurring daily. The process of bankruptcy of these lands goes steadily on. The rate of reversion is about 3,000 acres a month.

Some of the land the Auditor-General resells—a very small proportion; some he trades for other lands of similar value in order to group up the state's holdings, but the great bulk of the increasing estate has gone into and continues to go into the hands of the Public Domain Commission.

Here is where the active work of "doing something" with the bankrupt lands of Michigan is going on. What this commission is doing, its plans and accomplishments, and the possibilities of accomplishment afford the outstanding, concrete example of what could and should be done with the entire 10.000,000 acres of idle land within the state. There, reclamation has begun. There it is planned to re-establish the forests of Michigan.

ARTICLE II.

By far the largest owner of bankrupt land in Northern Michigan is the state.

The state, as landlord, at this time has title in a million acres, in round numbers. The amount varies from day to day, as lands revert for taxes and trades are made to consolidate the public holdings. The greater part of this state-owned territory has been organized into a public domain. Lands in the public domain are not on sale, except to round out and perfect its geographical organization. The greater part of Michigan's landed estate is therefore out of the market.

Most of the privately-owned land where bankrupt or near bankrupt acreage prevails is on the market, but not much is being sold now, except for grazing. Traveling northward, making inquiries as to land ownership as you go, you will find that the size of individual and corporate holdings increase. In the Upper Peninsula a trifle more than 30 concerns own 6,000,000 acres.

Lands in general are being spoken of—timber lands, potential farming lands, grazing lands and waste lands. There are two or three corporations on this side of the Straits which appear to have title in acreages that aggregate as much as some of the large Upper Peninsula holdings. There are many persons who would like to know just how much, and also how much of each kind of land. There is the United States Government's Agricultural Department, for instance, more especially the Forestry Bureau. A Congressional resolution, originating with Senator Arthur Capper, calls on the Forestry Department to find out how much standing timber is left in this country. The department has been trying. The result in Michigan has been similar to the result achieved by investigators from the University of Michigan and by The News scout, who followed the trail up into the State Assessors' office. All these visitors were asking the same questions.

DEAL IN DESCRIPTIONS.

To the questions about ownership and extent of ownership this was the answer: The field books of the assessors contain the information. but it never has been assembled. Getting it in form to answer the questions would mean the work of several relatively expert persons for several weeks.

What the assessors deal with is descriptions, not names of owners. in their formulated records. While tax levies are made on individuals and corporations in their names, they get a bill, not for their whole properties but for parts according to descriptions numbering hundreds for some owners. Segregation and assembling of these areas according to ownership, with illuminating notes as to the character of the lands—timbered, cut over, swamp or what not—would be valuable information and the assessors are quite willing to let anyone who wants it come and take it. The men from the United States Forestry Department took a look, proclaimed the value of the data in the field books, said they ought to have the material in assembled form, and that they might be back. That was months ago and they have not returned.

In the assessors' office the opinion prevails that the information would be valuable for the state—especially since there seems to be a remarkable new and growing interest in Michigan's one-time timber lands, now waste lands. Not only the foresters but the soil men of the University and colleges, the development bureaus and persons of forward-looking tendencies generally are beginning to ask fundamental questions about those lands.

U. OF M. SEEKS ACTION.

They want to know what denudation of North Michigan lands has to do with lumber costs and the shortage of houses in big towns and little, and they want to know why fence posts are costing so much in a "timber state," and so on. But assembling these facts as to ownership of lands in detail, as to the precise character rather than the market value only, of the lands and their hereditaments, is no part of the state assessors' business. They haven't any appropriation for such work. They think the matter might well be attended to.

But one concrete suggestion was encountered in a rather lengthy inquiry into this matter. It appears that the University of Michigan extension department, sensing the interest in and importance of this nation-wide inquiry into forest products and the forest industry, wants to do something. If money could be found to finance the job, the assessors at Lansing would be more than willing to let the skilled students the University sends out have the use of the field books. It seems to be up to the University Board of Regents.

Outside of areas which the state acquired from Government land grants in the old days, and virtually all of which went long since in sales to lumbermen and homesteaders, and grants to educational institutions, the state's land as we find them today, the million acres spoken of at the beginning of this article, are lands forfeited to the state since 1893, when the state tax homestead law went into effect.

MANY ACRES FORFEITED.

By operation of this law, turning back to the state land once deeded to private persons but on which they failed to pay taxes, a total of 2,300,000 acres have passed through the auditor-general's hands. He has resold to homesteaders since 1895 a total of 445,798 acres. So much for the first effort of the colonizer and land developer to develop for agriculture and allied industries the cut-over lands left by the lumberman. How well it succeeded in the palmy development days may be judged from the fact that 190,598 acres were later forfeited to the state again for non-payment of taxes. Homesteaders retain title to this day in the remaining 255,200 acres.

The reversions that are going on now, adding to the state's ownership land at the rate of 3,000 acres a month come, some of them, from these retained homesteads, but the largest part now, as formerly, from the old-time lumber companies or their successors who are holding their cut-over lands hoping—for what, who knows? Exploitation for agriculture grows annually less hopeful, and yet prices for cut-over lands are rising. If you ask why, the answer is that, still hoping to sell, the owner must double his sale price every 10 years to catch up with his tax outlay and the compounded interest on his investment.

The state lands are in the hands of the auditor general, as "land agent." He sells when he can, trades with other Governmental owners when they have land the state wants, and turns the rest over to the Public Domain Commission to run as a business undertaking for the state.

REPLANTING IS TASK.

He has turned over the 650,000 acres spoken of above, and adds to it virtually all of the 3,000 acres that are coming in every month. The Public Domain Commission, like the auditor-general with the residue of the state lands, carries on a business of buy, sell and barter, to consolidate its holdings and organize them for business administration. The real business of the commission is to conserve what resources are found to have been left by the former owners and trying to reclaim the land—protecting what forest growth exists and replanting the forests that 'have been devastated.

Two things are to be considered in connection with this big public estate of 650,000 acres. One is that while there is some good land scattered on it, it is the poorest land in Michigan. The other fact of note is that it pays taxes, every acre of it.

It is the poorest land in Michigan as a matter of course. It is the land made up in largest part of homesteads and cut-over lumber lands which couldn't afford to pay taxes five years in succession and was allowed to revert. It is bankrupt land in the real meaning of the word. That is the broad fact. There are comparatively large areas of good land in the public domain, some of it, as will later be shown, capable of yielding today thousands of dollars to the state treasury from sale of standing timber.

OPPOSITION AT FIRST.

Good or bad, as stated, all pay taxes. The reason for this throws a vivid light on conditions under which the would-be regenerators of the bankrupt lands would have to work. Up to 1917 there was opposition all through the north country to the policy of turning these bankrupt acres over to the Public Domain Commission for withdrawal from the market. At first it was the local patriots and the exploiters, joining chorus in the chant that the lands ought to be sold by the auditor-general and "the farmers given a chance to develop" them. Latterly the chances of getting farmers on to such land becoming more and more remote, the opposition centered on the true-enough claim that withdrawal of these lands would mean that the counties in which they were located never would derive any tax money from them—a genuine hardship in the poorer counties and a valid-enough argument, in spite of the fact that the lands in question had reverted because they did not pay taxes. They might, some time.

The argument was wiped out at the legislative session of 1917 by enactment of a law which requires the Public Domain Commission to pay a tax of 5 cents an acre on all its holdings, and of this amount the counties having public domain lands get their share. What helped to enact this law was a provision in it that the money so derived must be used for the construction of highways. If there is anything these interior northern counties dote on it is highways. They need them.

PUBLIC PAYS TAXES.

So the public pays taxes on its North Michigan domain, whether some of the other fellows do or not. Next, naturally, we want to know about income—and here we are, again, back on the main track. We will hardly need to be told that the public domain is not earning its taxes, much less earning anything for the public—not at this time. What we want to know is, what are our representatives on the job doing to make the proposition pay out—taxes anyhow, with a view to net income sometime? That is the main track spoken of.

Answering that question, one must of necessity at the same time furnish facts that will answer the larger questions about the conditions and prospects of the whole 10,000,000 acres of bankrupt lands, among which lie the acres of the state domain. Remember that the public domain is a sample of the whole—worse land, but better administered, as probably will be agreed when the facts are set forth. The conditions of the country and the problems of the people on the land, as also the problems of the people on the undeveloped lands and in the towns and cities, of all Michigan, in support of whatever remedial measures may be adopted, are practically the same whether the lands be public or private.

The forces that operated to make bankrupt the lands the state owns are still operating. They are forcing into bankruptcy millions more of acres which the state, if it doesn't look out, may become the owner of, as Sinbad "owned" the Old Man of the Sea.

PROBLEMS ARE GIGANTIC.

The job of putting a stop to or at least mitigating the force of operation of these bankrupting causes is the same on the private lands as the public lands; as also the problem of restoring the lands to use and profit once correction is affected.

These problems are concrete. They are reality itself, and they are gigantic, some of them. There is one, among the most important, that might not occur to any one considering the reclamation of disused lands as a land and crop problem, merely. Off hand, it might be said: well, there is the land, poor quality, of course, nothing on it much that is marketable—the problem is to make things grow on it that will pay. But that is not where the problem begins for the forward-looking men who have the reclamation of the bankrupt acres of Northern Michigan at heart.

The simile of a location for the re-establishment of a business would line up closer to fact if not vacant land, but a factory building were conceived. If it were a factory building to be re-equipped and set going, but which stood disused, vacant and but little watched, this one necessity would instantly occur to mind: what we have, the vacant building, must first be protected.

That is the case with the northern lands. About a third of our potential "forest factory" is fire-swept every five to six years. When he gets all the facts an average person would inquire with some impatience, what's the use of talking about beginning to re-establish the forest industry on the old-time forest lands when what is left is liable to be burned? The answer would have to be: very little use, indeed.

DESTROYS LAND'S VIRILITY.

And the man having knowledge of what a real forest fire really does would wonder what the impatient one would say if he knew, as Mr. Lovejoy in preceding articles has stated, that the fires not only burn the growth on the lands, but burn up the land itself, its virility, making it little by little, a desert more and more incapable of reclamation.

The forest fire menace is the hurdle on the threshold of the waste land problem. This can be proved by telling what the fires have done to make so much of north Michigan bankrupt, what they are still doing, and what, possibly, can be done about it.

ARTICLE III.

There are men now living, men who don't admit that they are old, who still have in their ears the screech of the circular saw that ripped through obese pine logs and yowled through dense forests that covered the lands which today appear in these chronicles as the "bankrupt lands of northern Michigan." For more than 20 years, that is, from 1870 to beyond 1890, Michigan led the world in lumber production, dropped second to Wisconsin in the next decade, and by the end of the following 10 years had dropped suddenly out of the list of eight important lumber, producing states of the union. The Southern pine industry had developed, and the Northwest coast industry was getting on its feet in those later years.

12 MILLION ACRES.

In Michigan, in the palmy days of lumbering and denudation of land, there were lumbered off or burned 12 million acres of pinery. The figure is given by Filibert Roth, head of the University of Michigan Forestry faculty. And at 15,000 feet of lumber to the acre this meant 180 billion feet—all pine; while 8 million acres of hardwood at 10 thousand board feet to the acre yielded 80 billion more. The total lumber logged OR BURNED in North Michigan the professor estimates at 260 billion feet, and as an estimator in this field of inquiry Prof. Roth, one quickly learns, has the reputation of being pre-eminent.

Loss by fire interests us just now. Fire has run neck and neck with the lumber operators in the wholesale job of devastating acres by the millions. Now the yowl of the circular saw is hushed in these lands, down to the merest murmur, the camps are "folded and gone," but the fires are not gone. They continue in the business of denudation and desert production.

ONE-THIRD BURNED.

While lumbering was active, and lumber towns flourishing, and railroads reaching tentacles farther and farther into the land to take in supplies and bring in the products of the camps and mills, fire was eating up, according to Prof. Roth's estimate, something less than 23 per cent of the timber which nature had set on the land. The lumbermen themselves commonly estimate the fire loss of those days to have been fully one-third.

The Michigan lumber cut today is not to be sniffed at, considering demands and prices—it is now about a billion feet a year, over $75,000,000 worth, taking the forest growth off 100,000 acres every twelve month, adding that much area every year to the millions of acres of stump lands now existing. These are Prof. Roth's figures again. What is left is very valuable indeed, and what could be put back would be much more valuable, both of which facts need to be borne in mind as bearing on the fire question. But what the fires did besides burning up about $1,200,000,000 worth of trees, reckoned on values of the time of the old days of lumbering, is really most important of all, and for this reason: What the fires did then in addition to burning timber they are doing to this day.

What they did, and continue to do, is to make absolute, complete and all but irretrievable the havoc wrought by the timber cutters. First take the superficial aspects of this moving picture of advancing desolation.

Towns dwindled when the timber stands receded before the saw and ax, and nothing industrial of equal consequence came in to take the place of lumbering. All native Michiganders, even in the largest cities, where live people who never saw a pine tree, know about that, realizing well the general effect. What is not so well realized is how completely the fires that crept over the devastated lands, through the "slashings" and through what timber tracts the first operations had left, completed the devastation begun by the lumbermen. Much less is it realized that besides burning the forest growth, virgin and second growth, the fires burned the soil itself.

Even a forest fire has something good about it. The greatest enemy of the bankrupt land area, second or even equal to the hurry-up lumber operator, has been fire; but fire also has been the servant of the farmer in clearing, and it has been the agency of nature in helping restock denuded lands. Fire that may destroy the seed of the remnant, solitary white pine, cooks the hard cone of the jack pine, pops out the seed and aids that species. for one, to propagate.

THE JACK PINE'S DAY.

This fire susceptibility of the white pine and fire resistance of the jack pine helps to account for the spread of the latter humbler and less valuable species on areas where once the majestic white pine flourished. But the once despised jack pine is not so despicable nowadays. Timber shortage and famine prices have brought him well forward in the esteem of men who once anathematized him.

Jack Pine on white pine land is a symptom of what the fires do to the soil. They do more than that. Just what, let Prof. Roth tell:

"Fires destroy the mulch of leaves, twigs and rotting limbs. The mulch varies from 500 pounds an acre in good jack pine to 2,000 pounds of leaves alone in a forest of beech and maple. The leaf fall of 1919 is, say, a ton per acre in a good stand. This is rotted and turned to leaf mold by 1923; the leaf mold of 1920, '21 and '22 meantime covering the ground as a layer of dead leaves, the more recent firm and dry on top. Insects, fungi, bacteria and worms are all at work and are necessary to good fertile soil. A heavy fire burns all this, often two to four inches down.

WOULD COST $10 AN ACRE.

"If this land were farmed at once the ashes would be too deep on much land, but on the whole would be of some help; but the mulch, the mold and the living things necessary to make this leaf mold are all gone. It would cost not less than $10 an acre to get this land back where it was, only as a good beginning; and it would take a number of years. The poorer the land the harder, the slower the recovery."

Here the professor, without having it exactly in mind, is talking about that million-acre estate of We, Us & Co. Ours is the poor land—poorest of all, the land "slowest to recover" from fire damage. We must remember this when we come to take account of what the administrators of our property are doing to protect us from fire and to restock our land.

When removal of the forest and the sawmills gave the average lumber town of North Michigan a jolt backwards, beginning along in the early '90s and continuing down to today; when fires came up through the slashings and the wasted lands that had grown up to scrub oak and poplar; and when they burned up many towns and drove their populations into the lakes or sent them flying, scorched and half naked, over the warped rails of the railroads, seeking for the safety they didn't always find, the fires had not done all their damage. Oscoda, in 1911, and Metz, five years before that, were tragedies so great that nobody can forget. A fugitive flat-car load of people, mostly women and children, burned to death near Metz. A steamer happening along just saved Oscoda's people, crowded on a wharf, while the town burned up. These are only episodes in a long tale of terror.

FERTILITY BURNED OUT.

But, more than this, these fires burned out the fertility of the land. Towns have dwindled, railroad spurs been taken up, homesteads abandoned, much else of decay and desolation wrought, not only because the lumber industry has gone, but because soil fertility, if not quite gone, is so badly impaired that it starves out the farmer. And when you starve out the farmer in a pioneer country you starve out the town and the railroad. You remember about the homesteaders on those 190,598 acres within what is now "our" landed estate—starved out and their farms become the property of the state? If that much territory drifted into starvation, you may well ask how much more towns and villages along with the farms have suffered from famine. If you asked, nobody would answer. Nobody could.

In the face of this lugubrious record, along comes, now, a proposition to restock with forest growth such of these devastated lands as are obviously and concededly not fit for agriculture. It must be evident to all readers that there are available for agriculture millions of acres more than are included in the public domain. That is, indeed, the proposition—to restock with forest growth much of this wasted acreage. It is necessary to come quickly to an understanding of what is meant by "restocking."

WHAT IS MEANT.

In the large, it means a proposal to begin to put back on the bankrupt and near-bankrupt acres the forest industry that once made it enormously wealth producing. And to put it back in a way not to furnish another single harvest as of yore, but as a permanent, established, self-perpetuating industry. "Putting it back" is another term that must be explained.

Restoring, replacing for perpetuity, in small or large degree, the forest industry of Michigan, restocking the idle lands with forest growth, means replanting as a part of the plan. Even more than that it means assisting nature to do the work herself. Forests may fall before the woodsman or go up in smoke, but the beneficent restorative offices of Mother Nature go on forever, if not wilfully allowed to be impeded.

Nature is doing her best to bring back to production vast areas of non-productive land in the region under consideration. As has been hinted in the passing remarks about the jack pine taking the white pine's place, she does not do her best work, doesn't replace No. 1 growth with No. 1, but with a poorer stock, unless she is assisted. The first help, and perhaps the greatest help, she gets in the North country is from the fire fighters—and their help isn't anything that it ought to be.

Consideration of the fire element in the general problem will not be complete without examining into the fire-fighting needs and performances on the 10,000,000 acres of idle lands.

ARTICLE IV.

Owners of the Michigan public domain, the citizens of Michigan, well may ask what is being done to control the fires which are burning the remnants of the state's forest wealth and gradually reducing to infertile mineral nakedness the soil on which the forests grew. They may well ask the question in its relation to the state's own domain of upwards to a million acres, and they can as legitimately ask it as pertaining to the other domain of more than 9,000,000 acres belonging to private persons.

For the land and forest question means food and housing for all along with multitudinous other things, such as ties for railroads, now lamentably deficient, constituting one of the big railway reconstruction problems; such as shoes, the leather of which must have its tanbark; such as newspapers, for they must have their pulpwood, growing on the stump—it is there that began the printed page which conveys to you at this moment the fundamental facts having to do with the fire menace on forest lands.

FIRE IS PERIL.

Something of the real importance of the forest industry which forward-looking men are trying to save and replenish, it is hoped, is beginning to dawn on the minds of persons who are too busy with immediate affairs to go back, and back, and back to the sources of things.

Control of fire in the woods and in the slashings, which are the stump lands strewn with the tops and branches of trees left by the lumbermen, would mean not only valuable property saved but property created. Just merely mitigating the fire evil would do much. What it would mean to many important industries and sources of the supply in the daily life of the citizen will be more fully indicated later, but take one of them which, naturally, the investigator into these things especially well remembers. Take pulpwood and the paper supply.

"If you will keep the fires out of the Michigan north woods for 10 years," Prof. Roth remarked during a conversation, "there will be 5,000,000 cords of wood pulp in those woods not existing today, and 5,000,000 cords of wood pulp is equal to the entire amount of wood pulp used in the United States in one year."

USES FOR PULP.

And newspaper use is not the only use for wood pulp. Pulp goes into paper mache, strawboard, wrapping paper, book paper and many other things. Mr. Roth, by his fire prevention program, would, in a sense, supply all these industries from the depleted Michigan forest lands alone.

On a large part of 15,000,000 acres of cut-over land lying idle in this state, he pointed out, there is more or less of a second growth, self-sown or self-sprouted, which will keep growing provided the fires do not destroy it. He includes 5,000,000 acres more than we have been dealing with; for there are cut-over lands in Michigan not rightly to be included in the 10,000,000 acres of bankrupt or near-bankrupt lands. If only 10,000,000 acres were to be converted into a real forest, however—that is, by planting where planting is needed, filling in the gaps left by voluntary seeding—these 10,000,000 acres would produce yearly the 5,000,000 cords of wood pulp needed, Mr. Roth added. Evidently he would include some hardwood lands of the Upper Peninsula, where there is much of his 15,000,000 acres of cut-over. Much of this better cut-over land about the state is first-class grazing ground. At that, it will be learned that dealing with OUR lands, the public domain, approximating results could be accomplished.

SPARK CREATES HAVOC.

The statistician's figures are interpreted as being somewhat larger than realizable in practice. Absolute control of forest fires—"keeping them out"—is not expected by foresters or anybody else. Nowhere in the world where forests grow, probably, is that possible. Relative control is possible, and is accomplished in places, such as parts of the United States Government forest reserves and the municipal and state-owned forests in European countries. Fires in the woods and on the sand plains of Upper Michigan there will always be, probably. A locomotive spark or a cigaret stub has been known to burn over an area equivalent to a county. Fires will start. Stopping them before they get far is what fire "control" in North Michigan means.

J. Girvin Peters, chief of the United States Forestry Department which co-operates with the Michigan and 23 other state governments in fighting forest fires, estimated in 1912 that an average of 10,000,000 acres are burned over annually in the United States, with a money loss of about $20,000,000. A sizable bonfire.

STATE'S FIRE LOSS.

Michigan's loss by forest fires for a period of 10 years ending in 1911, is declared in a circular of the Forest Fire Protective department of the Michigan Hardwood Manufacturers' Association, to have been $20,000,000. Of the annual loss, then, for a 10-year period, Michigan's loss was one-tenth of the total for the country—all out of proportion when one remembers that in these latter years Michigan's timber wealth per acre does not approach that of western states which come in the reckoning.

And note that these losses are of timber values only. Loss by soil depreciation and because of the starving out of the farmers and town dwellers dependent on forest or agricultural harvest is given no place in the totals. Nor even is the damage to young stands of timber and growth well begun but too young to be called timber, reckoned in. The figures are for losses in timber merchantable as such at the time of estimate.

Setting aside statements of values, of dizzying heights, take areas. An average of half a million acres is burned over in Michigan every year. The two active fire seasons are spring and autumn, spring the worst, though this is not understood generally. The reasons will appear when the details of forest fire fighting are given. One of J. Girvin Petters' men, who was here during the bad fire season of 1919, reported back to his chief that "at least a half a million acres have burned over in Michigan to date," and the date was in midsummer, with the fall fires to come.

ESTIMATE BURNT AREA.

Half a million acres for every year may be argued against as too large an estimate, but considering that there have been many "bad" years equal to or worse than 1919, that there has been in time past more to burn and less protection even than now, and that the effort to minimize the facts of destruction has been stronger in the past than it is now, the belief is that an estimate of 500,000 acres of fire in this state for every year is not too large. That is the area of an average Lower Peninsula county, burned over yearly. The fires have burned every year for the last half century. Of course many of the same acres burn over, again and again. It is, in fact, repeated fires on the same land that work the real havoc.

You will want to be told at once, if you do not know, what is being done about it. The forest fire fighting organization, its operation, the cost, the results accomplished and what might reasonably be expected to be accomplished—these subjects are of first importance in considering what should be done to make Michigan's bankrupt acres, state and private owned, remunerative.

TWO FOREST FIRES EACH YEAR.

The state maintains two forest fire departments, both under the control of the Public Domain Commission. There is one for a part of the state's own domain, another for North Michigan outside of that area.

About half of the state's domain has been set aside as forest land reservations, called in the vernacular of officialdom "state forests," though large parts of them are as bald as an Arctic waste. There are about 325,000 acres in the Forest Reserve system, and 156,258 acres in the eight forests that have been "opened," to date. The opening plan now contemplates two new forests every year; so that, while the plan has not been fully carried out, the number of state forests and the number of acres in each of the opened forests is continually increasing. "Opening" a state forest consists of marking its boundaries, putting up a house and a barn, also a watchtower or two, stringing telephone lines, and beginning construction of fire lines and setting out trees.

FORESTER IS WARDEN.

Over the state forest the state forester is fire warden, and on his domain the other state organization has nothing to do. The other organization contends with forest fires over the rest of Northern Michigan. This is one of the departments of a department subordinate to the Public Domain Commission, the State Game, Fish and Forest Fire Department.

Forest fire fighting in both departments goes along with something else, in the case of the state forest part of the public domain it goes with propagation of forests, and in the case of the millions of acres outside the state forests, both public and private lands, it goes with propagation of fish and game and enforcement of the game laws. Secretary George L. Lusk of the Public Domain Commission is the fire chief, leader of both fire wardens.

The state maintains a fire department to fight fires on private lands for the same reason that fire departments are maintained in cities, because property protection is a public function and duty. The beneficiaries are taxed, of course. There are two private fire fighting organizations among timber owners, but both moribund.

Fire fighting on that part of the public domain included in the forest reserves is a very different business from fighting fires over the millions of acres outside—the problem on the state's own land which has been organized for use can be and is dealt with differently than that on widespread land, more than nine-tenths of which is privately owned. It appears to be a more difficult problem. At all events, State Forester Marcus Schaaf appears to have better control of the situation than the state fire warden and his men.

COUNTIES ARE GROUPED.

These latter have the job set for them of protecting not only most of the 10,000,000 acres of bankrupt and near-bankrupt lands but millions of acres of contiguous lands which, some of them, are of very great value because of standing timber on them. Indeed, there is yet a substantial notion prevalent among these fire fighters that protection of standing timber is their main job, if not their only job. You can hardly expect the average deputy fire warden or his helpers to admit the high cost of destruction of soil by fire until the fact has been called to his attention forcibly.

For fighting fires in the vast territory outside the state forests, the 36 counties in the forest fire area have been grouped by Fire Warden John Baird into 10 divisions; each a fire district in charge of a deputy fire warden, who lives somewhere in his district. Assisting the 10 deputy fire wardens are 39 special men, apportioned among the districts, and one inspector of railroad rights of way for the whole territory. These men serve all the year round. To these 50 men add, for the fire season, 42 game and fish wardens on the regular payroll who are instructed to give especial attention to forest fire fighting in the season. All are under direct command of the State Fish, Game and Forest Fire Commissioner.

COST OF FIRE FORCE.

This completes the standing fire fighting force to contend with fires raging sporadically over an area four times the size of Massachusetts, and burning on the average every year an area equal to a common sized county. Burning in spite of the fire fighters and the fire fighting. When fires rage large or become epidemic, casuals are called out for the emergency, and the state and townships jointly foot the bill.

This leads to a consideration of the finances of fire fighting and begins to let the light in on the question, what might, as a matter of plain business, be spent on this work.

ARTICLE V.

The plain evidence of the records is that Michigan's forest fire-fighting business has suffered because of its partnership with the state's game department. It has been subordinated. That is the fact obvious to a person looking at the whole situation with an eye keen for property values.

Without minimizing the worth of fish and game propagation, it will be found, when the balance is struck, that the sportsman's interests are accounted a very large figure in the total.

By comparison forest fire protection in North Michigan shows up scantily beside game protection.

ONLY 50 FIREMEN.

The state provides the State Fire Warden, who is also Fish and Game Warden, with 50 men as a standing fire protection force. And the area which these 50 men must "protect" is that from the north line of the counties of Arenac-to-Mason up to the straits, across the straits and westward through the Upper Peninsula to the Wisconsin border. You could set New Hampshire, Vermont, Massachusetts and Connecticut down on top of that territory and not much of them would get wet.

In the fire season 42 fish and game wardens turn in to help the firemen, but they have their fish and game laws to enforce meantime.

This is the skeleton organization, filled in when crises arise by impressment of help from the towns and farms. It should be added that there are—or were last season—eight horsemen of the State Constabulary operating from one point over one of the worst areas; out of Pellston and through the northwest counties of the Lower Peninsula, acting as rangers to enforce the fire laws, educate the public and give warning of incipient fires. Every township supervisor is also, by effect of the forest fire protection law of 1903, a fire warden. They are seen at their height of action, as a rule, when it comes to drumming up volunteers for emergency fire fighting.

MICHIGAN'S FIRE IDEA.

It is plain at once that Michigan's forest fire fighting idea seems to be, basically, to have a small force of men widely dispersed over a vast area, to raise the cry of "fire!" when the fire gets going and rally the bucket brigade. The bucket brigade is no slouch, either. For a mob organization it has done enormous work. The forestry statisticians have taken pencil and paper and figured it all out, on the basis of days' work at the going rate per day, multiplied into the reported and estimated numbers of up-state natives who have labored in heat and smoke to save themselves and their neighbors.

"In 1918 and 1919 they did free work they would not have done for $8,000,000 in pay," says Prof. Roth.

The most ardent of forest and forest land protection advocates have no idea of arguing for a force of regular forest fire fighters that would take the place of any such public co-operation as this—rather, to provide a standing force that would inspire the natives to greater effort of co-operation, because of its visible proof that the state recognizes the size of the problem, the danger to lives and property, and its determination to quit shirking its own share of the labor and cost.

WHAT PEOPLE WANTED.

Many things could be set down in explanation of the meagerness of Michigan's professional forest fire protection organization and the way it works.

In the first place, this organization is exactly what the people of Michigan, through their Legislature, have said they want. Warden Baird has just demoted the deputy state warden, William J. Pearson, of Boyne Falls, who for years had charge of the district deputy wardens. There is no place in the law for a deputy state warden. Pearson was appointed and his job laid out by William R. Oates, who was Mr. Baird's predecessor.

Last year was so bad a fire year up north, so much burned that, with the growing interest in forestry and waste land matters, the forest fire protection department evidently began to get apprehensive. They are reorganizing; and in so doing they are falling back on the letter of the law which gives them being. The 10 district wardens are hereafter to work under the authority and control of the State Fish, Game and Forest Fire Warden—Mr. Baird.

MORE ARE NEEDED.

More needs to be done than this. The state warden and his men will need help. In the last analysis the Legislature and the public are responsible.

This last statement is to make widely known conditions and necessities, changes in laws, and additions to appropriations. The fire fighters hustle around on their vast job, accomplishing a great deal, but overwhelmed by the size of the job, nevertheless; and they are quite willing to explain their troubles, if you take the trouble to ask. As for finding among themselves a man who can and will stand up before the Legislature and tell the people of Michigan what they ought to know about this business, and boldly state the necessities of the case in dollars and cents—well, as public educators, they are pretty good fire fighters.

One senses rather than finds in tangible substance the fact of the subordination of fire fighting to game interests. To one coming into the state warden's office from days and weeks in the up-state forests and slash lands and isolated farms on the clay oases in the sand country, the old, old fallacies about the woods and the clearings are clearly perceptible, lurking in shadowy corners. All these people are Michigan men, most of them native to the soil of the barren lands or next door neighbors—steeped in the traditions of the north country.

"The early settler regarded the forest as a foe to be conquered. It impeded agriculture, and it harbored wild beasts," said Orlando F. Barnes the other day. He is chairman of the State Board of Tax Commissioners, and was discussing laws that are inimical in their effects to the restoration of forests on bankrupt lands.

It is not fanciful to suspect that the age-old tradition has its operative effect in the Michigan forest fire protection organization.

JUST ANOTHER ASPECT.

And there is another fact, especially appealing to the official mind. The game department pays its own way; the fire protection department, naturally, does not. Every dollar spent educating the northwoods public in how not to start fires, every dollar spent stopping the fires when they start by act of man or act of Providence in sending a lightning bolt on an old and dry jack pine or a heap of slash, has to come from the Legislature, that is from the taxpayer. And if the public official, on the average, isn't modest about asking for money, he is at least cautious about what he asks it for. And so long as so few people realize how penny-wise and pound-foolish it is to let the north country burn, just so long, undoubtedly, will the forest fire protection arm of the state government hesitate to make its legitimate monetary needs known.

Its legitimate money needs are known, at least have been figured out by one man having as good knowledge of the whole problem as any man in Michigan. Prof. Roth has done it. Besides being one of the world's foremost teachers of forestry, he has been Michigan's forester in years past, planted with his own hands waste areas up in Roscommon and Crawford counties and along the Au Sable River.

HAS PREPARED FIGURES.

He has prepared figures for a forthcoming report of the Public Domain Commission. In Prof. Roth's calculated study of the problem the citizen who foots the bills will have something clear, concise and determinative to go by.

Before Prof. Roth's figures are presented it remains to be told what the fire protection organization is getting now. The report of the game, fish and forest fire commissioner, in the Public Domain Commission report for 1916-18, covers eleven and two-thirds pages for game, and has a one-page summary for the forest fire report. Turning back to the biennial report preceding, one finds eight pages in the fire report—six pages of tables giving dates, areas and damage wrought by fires, and costs of extinguishment. From July 1, 1914, to June 30, 1916, what fires were put out and didn't burn out, did $8,276 damage in the Upper Peninsula, and cost $2,743.45 to put out; in the Lower Peninsula they did damage, according to this report, of $24,827 and cost $6,842 to extinguish. In the 1916-18 period the cost to put out fires totals $12,808. Putting out fires is small part of the fire fighters' work. They have to patrol the lands, post notices, put up towers and phone lines for watchmen, and do many other things.

EXACT COST LACKING.

The exact total cost of forest protection, outside of the public domain devoted to state forests, is impossible to get at, because the accounts are mixed with the fish and game accounts, as is natural, the same men doing the same work in the same department.

The one definite figure obtainable is in the Auditor-General's report, where there is an item, "forest fires, paid for suppression of," and this item, in the report of 1918, is $43,434.66. This is the amount for the fiscal year ending June 30, 1918, and it includes the two-thirds of the aggregate amount paid by the state as days' wages to emergeney fire fighters, the township paying the other third.

More particularly how the money was spent will appear in the comparison that will be printed later along with Prof. Roth's estimate of what should be spent.   •

ARTICLE VI.

Michigan spends $50,000 a year putting out forest fires. More is spent in addition maintaining the skeleton forest and forest land protection organization on the millions of acres needing protection and which lie outside the otherwise protected areas, of the state forests, under the management of the Public Domain Commission. The $50,000 plus, is expended by the State Game, Fish and Forest Fire Department. The plus amount, spent for maintenance of the standing organization and its equipment, never reaches $100,00 in a single year.

Michigan gets off cheaply. It does until one comes to reckon up the fire damage and balance it against the expenditure. An ordinary business corporation would fire a general manager who boasted about how little fire hose he caused to be bought in a year, when the opposite page of the ledger carried an account of fire loss that was over 27 times the cost of hose bought. That is what forest fire "protection" and forest fire damage amount to in Michigan, from the comparative point of view.

The annual loss of merchantable timber has been in recent years $2,00,000 a year, timbermen say in formal reports. Add to this a modest estimate of soil damage, of $5 an acre—Prof. Roth's figure—and you would have to add to these estimates another big figure for damage done to second growth, not yet large enough for commercial use, but stock in hand, just as much so as calves and colts on a livestock farm. This last figure nobody has mentioned, so far as known. When you add them all together and balance them against the $50,000 to $100,000 investment in fire fighting you quickly perceive that the investment is so small that you wonder the waste has been allowed to go on so long. The answer is that so few people have had the facts.

EUROPE'S FORESTS PAY.

Forest protection is better in Europe, where they have state and municipal tracts of woodland that pay revenues to the public.

There they began restoring forests 200 years ago and have in some countries kept pace with forest devastation. In the better administered areas, as in Saxony, forest protection costs from 15 to 30 cents an acre. These forests pay not only expenses but a profit into the public treasury.

For Michigan, which is just beginning the work of forest reclamation, money for protection will have to be invested, and the state will have to wait upon rehabilitation of existing forests and growth of new forests to get its money back—and wait still longer for profits. But a beginning can not be made without spending money for adequate protection of what now exists and what is being brought into existence.

It requires an outlay of 5 cents an acre on a 15,000,000-acre area, requiring protection. It will cost, in fact, 10 cents an acre adequately to protect the 10,000,000 of idle cut-over lands and the 5,000,000 acres which are not idle but timber stocked. Five of the 10 cents for each acre, however, will be furnished half the protection, at least, at no cost to the state. Timber owners have their own protection organizations; mills shut down and whole towns turn out when there are big fires. The public comes in without expectation of repayment when the job is at its worst and costs the most.

$550,000 NECESSARY.

"If the state will spend $500,000 a year on organization and improvements, the next bad fire season will not find the people unprepared and helpless," says Prof. Roth.

A detailed estimate of the cost that should be paid out by the state, independent of private help, and aiming to encourage co-operative effort on the part of the public, by Prof. Roth, exceeds his offhand estimate by $50,000. Here is Mr. Roth's summary of "a reasonable, practical minimum for effective fire protection in Michigan annually to be expended for the next 20 years":

State Fire Warden, at $6,000 and expenses	$ 10,000
30 County Wardens, at $2,000 and expenses	90,000
Supervisors as Wardens, at $100	40,000
500 special Wardens, at $200	100,000
Clerks, printing, etc	10,000
Improvements, equipment, etc.	200,000
Fire fighting, extra help, ordinary years	100,000
Total	$550,000

For emergency years, a special standing fund of $500,000 for fire fighting.

WOULD LEVY TAX.

To raise this money, Prof. Roth would have the state levy a special tax of two cents an acre on all cut-over lands not part of actual farms; a special tax of five cents an acre on all standing timber, and apportion to the forest protection fund a part of all gun and hunting license money. Generally, he says, this would yield the following returns for forest protection:

Tax on cut-over lands (10,000,000 acres)	$200,000
Tax on standing timber (4,000,000 acres)	200,000
Part of game protection fund, etc	150,000
Total	$550,000

A special tax on land for forest protection is no innovation, he points out. It has been in effect in Oregon since 1913. Voluntary organizations of timber owners in all the timbered states pay acre assessments, some of them as high as 25 cents an acre, where timber lands are especially valuable and protection difficult. The average assessment runs from five to ten cents an acre.

URGES EDUCATION.

Prof. Roth says educative work in forest protection should begin in earnest. The public should be fully informed what fires in the Northland mean in loss of forest products, deterioration of soil, de-

—29—

struction to animal life, loss in revenues derived from the patronage of sportsmen, and loss in revenues that might be derived from tourist traffic and resorters were the country saved from fire and made more attractive. More specifically, in the application of dollars to the problem, he says, supervisors should continue as fire wardens, on definite yearly pay, as stated in the table above. He would have a fire warden for each county and 30 wardens in the fire area, instead of the 10 district wardens, as now. He would pay them about what the district wardens are getting now.

He would have the state warden at Lansing empowered to employ at least 500 patrolmen, or rangers, which is the meaning of "special wardens" in the table. These would be men selected, so far as possible, among the local populations and would serve when called out. More fire towers and phones and some fire lines to break up the most dangerous bodies of slash are also comtemplated in the program. There are now three fire towers standing in the vast area of the fire country, and two or three more ready to go up, according to information furnished at the state warden's office. There are no fire lines whatever on this vast territory outside the state forests.

RESTOCK WITH TREES.

A proposal to spend $550,000 a year for forest protection, outside the 650,00 acres of the public domain, the most of which the State Forester will protect at a separate cost, will appeal to some Michigan citizens as too much, to some others as none too much, depending on the point of view. The point of view of some who think the figure looks large may shift a little with further consideration of what the financial returns are for protection investment. It is always to be borne in mind that the proposition is to take a first step necessary to reclamation of the idle lands by restocking them with trees: Propagation of forests by assistance to nature is not conceivable without protection. All authorities, state and national, have said that many times.

P. S. Lovejoy, co-laborer with Prof. Roth, in the University of Michigan forestry department, whose comprehensive article led this series, has written of "Timber Values as Affected by Fire Hazard." He speaks only of one of the elements of value to be reckoned on when waste lands are made to grow forests. That is merchantable timber.

FIRES IRREPARABLE.

"A burned factory," he points out, "can be rebuilt; a burned forest cannot be replaced"—meaning, not without great lapse of time. Hence forest fires do what is relatively irreparable damage. Hence it must rationally be expected that forest protection will cost more in proportion to assessed valuation at any given date than will fire insurance on a building or a business.

Forest insurance cannot be purchased in this country.

Insurance charges buy indemnification for losses and replacement of burned property. As has been explained, the system won't apply where there can be no replacement of the burned property—or at least the insurance companies take that view. The argument is, therefore, that it must be expected that forest protection will cost more than insurance. Protection must be raised to the highest possible point of efficiency to avoid irrecoverable losses.

It will not strike the average reader that to put $550,000 a year into protection instead of less than $100,000 in the effort to cut down an annual loss in timber, second growth and land values easily approximating $3,000,000 a year, is such a steep proposition. It will look even less when it is reflected that something must be done to make recreation of the forest a really practicable undertaking.

MOST FOR PROTECTION.

J. Girvin Peters, of the United States forest service, he who has charge of co-operation with the states, says:

"It is significant that many states whose forest work was begun mainly along experimental lines are now giving the larger part of their time and their appropriation for forestry to fire protection."

More money for the fire fighters to work with is not the only thing needed—they need sme changes in these laws. Nothing radical appears to be desired. Nobody is advocating divorcement of the state fire warden's office from the state game warden's office. There are too mny good arguments for keeping them together. The administrative work is much th same, the territory is the same, and the ultimate aim is the same—conservation of the state's resources and building them up. Game protection involves forest protection; the only wonder is that the game protectors do not seem to realize how necessary are forests to game interests.

NEED BETTER LAWS.

There are laws in some states requiring every timber owner to provide a patrol system satisfactory to the state authorities. Otherwise the state provides it and taxes the owner for it. Michigan's two private co-operative forest protection organizations, one in the Upper and one in the Lower Peninsula, are not as active, of recent years, as formerly.

Slash disposal laws are better defined and more effective in some states than in Michigan. In this state, while the forest fire protection law provides that the state fire warden and his men "may enter upon lands and remove or destroy brush, and other dangerous combustible material wherever necessary," there is nowhere in the vast fire area perceptible any systematic purpose or effort to reduce the fire hazard at this, its starting point. It appears that the "may" of the statute might well be made to read "shall."

Laws penalizing careless and malicious setting of fires that spread and cause great damage may be adequate enough, as statutes, but they are not enforced with anywhere near the vigor that the game laws are enforced. The records of prosecutions stand easily 10 to 1 in favor of the game laws.

STILL WASTE TIMBER.

Harvesting of timber goes on in this state. The cut approximates 1,000,000 feet of hardwood a year, and 100,000 acres are being added every year to the millions of acres of cut-over lands. And one hears all through the North tales of shiftless practices by lumbermen that rival tales of the older days—tops and branches left lying, in quite the fashion that the old-timers created the burnt-over slash lands all over the North Country. Some states have laws regulating the cutting of timber on private lands, and it appears on the face of it that if Michigen were to put up $550,000 or anything like that for fire protection, laws to make the slash makers take more care than they do would be well justified.

There are other legal matters to be considered, as well as the tax laws. One at least of which operates with the force of a law of nature to discourage the attempts of private owners to re-grow forests; but that is a subject that pertains rather to restoration of forests than to their destruction, and will be treated of when reforestation is taken up.

Having considered something of the necessities preliminary to the problem of restocking the idle acres it remains to be found out what is being done and can be done to restock. The point of attack for that study is logically the forest reservations of the Public Domain Commission, where beginnings have been made, and to that area of the inquiry, the state forests, we now return.

ARTICLE VII.

On millions of acres outside the state forests the problem first to be faced, as we have seen, is reduction of the fire menace as an assistance to nature in her efforts to reproduce the useful trees, later to assist nature by planting.

On the 650,000 acres allotted to the Public Domain Commission for state forest reservations, the fire problem is well in hand, by contrast with conditions outside. Nature is being given her chance, and, more, nature is being assisted. The whole program is to restore to the millions of acres of devastated lands up north the forest industry. About $55,000 a year is being spent to this end.

AN INFANT INDUSTRY.

Remember that you are about to scrutinize an infant industry. So infantile that you are asked to examine the industry in the very makings of it, from practically nothing. It will be found to have some of the puny, weakling aspects of a thing newly born. It is only about 15 years old in this state. It will be 45 years longer growing out of adolescense; for it takes on the average 60 years for such a tree as those planted by the state forester to reach a size that makes a lumberman, covetous. The pulpwood man and the chemical wood man, not to mention the barrel and box men and a host of others who can make money scavenging forests, will be coming down on our youthful forests long before the 60-year term is up. They are finding much now in protected forest areas, and they would find much more in 10 to 15 years if fires were kept out.

Of the Public Domain Commission's 650,000 acres only 156,158 acres have to date been organized as a forest reserve. One has to put in that "only," for large as the aggregate state forests are, one can not forget that 100,000 acres of cut-over are being added to the idle land area of this state every year.

The state forest domain is in eight forests. The newest one was "opened" last summer. That is the Pigeon River reserve, in south central Cheboygan county. "Opening" a state forest, as has been elsewhere mentioned, consists in running the exterior boundary lines, putting up living quarters for the forester's men, a barn, at least one watchtower, telephone lines, then beginning construction of fire lines and planting.

The other seven state forests, named in the chronological order of their opening, are: Higgins Lake, Houghton Lake, Fife Lake, Lake Superior, Ogemaw, Presque Isle, Alpena. There is, besides, a tract of virgin white pine, Interlochen State park, in Grand Traverse county, where the state forester gets much seed, but does not pursue reclamation activities.

FORESTS SPREAD OVER STATE.

The eight state forests mentioned are widely dispersed through the barren lands, and they are of diverse areas. The Lake Superior forest, on the north shore of Luce County and beginning about 20 miles west of Whitefish bay, runs westward to the Alger County line in a strip 30 miles long and six miles deep. It is the largest, embracing over 62,000 acres. The Ogemaw forest, just above West Branch—the Michigan Central railroad line, is the smallest—4,200 acres. A "map of the state forests," issued by the Public Domain Commission, neatly spotted in blue to show the forest areas, shows 74 of these, one of them down as far as Gratiot County; but this map reflects plans and aspirations, not performances. The eight largest areas have been opened. The others will be, some time, and they will be larger than they now are. The commission is constantly making deals to extend the forest reserve lines and to buy out such private parties as own little tracts within the confines of all the areas.

If you ever take it into your head to have a look at the Michigan enterprise of reclothing the barren lands with forests, the place to begin is at the Higgins Lake reserve. Here are field headquarters. Here is the state nursery, and the field office of the state forester. His business office is in Grayling, 12 miles distant.

The ride from the railway station, past the state military reservation at Portage Lake, is over graveled roads about half the way, then over the typical sand roads of the cut-over country. The end of the road is a group of modern buildings on the shore of Higgins Lake—a crystal clear body of water nine miles long and three miles wide, its shoreline sparsely pre-empted by resorters, as yet, but gaining yearly in popularity.

The largest building at forestry headquarters is the two-story cement block residence of the custodian, electric lighted and steam heated. All the buildings requiring it have running water. A hydraulic ram operating in a swale between the reservation buildings and the lake shore, where a spring creek has been dammed to form a pond in front of headquarters, supplies the buildings here and the nursery, back from the lake a couple of minutes' walk.

Each of the opened forests has a resident custodian. The custodian at the Higgins Lake reserve is also superintendent of the nursery.

SUPPLIES ALL FORESTS.

This nursery is the source of supply of seeding trees for all the forests. It also supplies seedlings at cost price to private persons, in lots of never less than 500 little trees. The nursery area is less than 30 acres, and the building is not much to look at—a mere shed; but the nursery grows seedling trees by the millions every year. The planting practice, on land wholly denuded, is to put in 1,700 seedlings to the acre. An acre with 50 full grown trees on it is a good "stand." The surplusage provided in planting is the allowance for loss by death, and the thinning processes pursued in silviculture—raising forests as a crop.

"It is high time that we began cropping our forest lands instead of mining them," as Orlando F. Barns recently remarked.

Artificial planting by the state began back in 1904, on a very small scale with the Higgins and the Houghton Lake reserves as the operating grounds. Prof. Roth was then in charge of the field work. The appropriation at that time was but $7,500 a year. By the close of the fiscal year 1918 the commission was expending $54,702 for all purposes on the seven forest reserves. In the last two years the opening of the Pigeon River Reserve has been the largest work. It cost, before the war, $6,000 to open a state forest. Now it costs $12,000 to $13,000.

"Forestry is a financial undertaking, pure and simple. It's got to be made to pay to succeed," State Forester Marcus Schaaf remarked to the writer while he was wandering around the reservation. And every minute of every day that one spends in watching the operations of Michigan's forestry department he is reminded of this point of view.

KNOWS VALUE OF TREES.

The forester looks upon his work as the labor of raising a crop of commercial wood products—lumber, pulp wood, chemical wood, ties, posts and poles, and all the rest. He knows the value of forest cover to animal life, appreciates the sportsman's and the tourist's interests, realizes the health and scenic value to a state's general population of living woods in place of barren lands; but when he reckons costs and places them alongside yields to decide whether he is making progress or not, he reckons in board feet and cords.

He doesn't even reckon in what is of most importance to the citizen wherever he lives. This is the value to the state of RE-ESTABLISHING ON IDLE LANDS AN INDUSTRY THAT HAS BEEN WIPED OUT, AND RE-ESTABLISHING IT IN PERPETUITY, that dying towns may come back to life, populations that are drifting away because employment is gone may find labor restored to them, a whole country blighted made new again.

Growing a forest is a long-time job, involving a large investment at a low rate of interest—from 2 to 3 per cent—and it is up to the forester to show that, aside from what may be called the general benefits to society, he must show financial benefit to the investor first of all.

Whatever may have been accomplished to date in this state in actual work, the state has a definite plan for the work, and it proves up successfully on the basis of the forester's severe reckoning—it must be shown that it pays.

Michigan's state forester has the problem of restocking what are virtually denuded lands. It has been pointed out before that this state-owned land, reverted to the state because of non-payment of taxes, is naturally the poorest land anywhere in the area of bankrupt acres.

"It is obvious that no receipts may be expected during the first 60 years," said Mr. Schaaf.

He was still speaking of commercial timber. There are small annual revenues all the time—from sale of nursery product, sale of second growth annually cut off in process of giving the most forward growth its chance to develop, and there is destined to be a larger revenue derivable from thinnings and forest scavenging as certain industries develop and needs increase. Pulp and paper makers are taking kinds of wood nowadays they snorted at a few years ago, and there is the chemical wood industry — using up small stuff from hardwood forests and turning out charcoal, acetate of lime and wood alcohol. Michigan leads all the states in this latter industry. But, says the state forester——

"It must be apparent to any reasonable minded person that the whole proposition is one in which the investor, in this case the state, must be willing to make considerable financial outlay and forego immediate returns for future profits. It is therefore a foregone conclusion that, starting with practically nothing, the expenditures accumulated during the first 60-year period, will be vastly in excess of the meager receipts that may be expected in the meantime. Such investments must be made in order to create and build up the working capital of the forest, and theoretically at least not until 1978, the first year of the second period of rotation, will a substantial output be realized and the investment begin to return interest. From that time forward, however, the returns will continue in perpetuity and in the same amount, so long as the forest working capital is not impaired."

REAL PROFIT BEGINS EARLY.

Mr. Schaaf was here dating his reckoning from 1917 and looking forward to the first harvest of completely matured timber at the end of 60 years. Sixty years would be a long time for the average citizen to look for returns on the tax money he is asked to put into a state forest industry. But the case isn't really quite as bad as that.

A recent special report of the forester carries tabular statements showing estimated outlay and estimated accretions of timber values, year by year, for the 60-year period and beyond. It becomes perfectly apparent to the layman studying these figures that this important fact lies buried in them.

The increment of value in the forest catches up with the total of increasing investment long before the 60 years expire. The 60 years mark the first harvest period—the first collection date, and when the harvest is realized it pays much more than the cost of production. Back in the years before that date lies the point where value represented in the still growing tree overlaps the cost of growing it. It is not harvested then, of course, because by not cutting it, it then begins to leave cost farther and farther behind in the race between cost and profit.

The rotation periods—in a sense harvesting periods—for forests are the same for all forests of similar tree population. The time element is fixed, but when it comes to the matter of actual dollars invested in a forest. the forest area has to come into the reckoning.

The state forester, in his calculations in his report, worked with a definite area in mind. This was 4,500 acres for each year. That is the planting plan of the Michigan Public Domain Commission, that many new acres of new planting to be added to the replanted areas in the state forests every 12 months. The performance has been less than 2,000 acres a year.

Two causes have operated to keep the planting operations down to a limit of less than half of what the commission wants to do, is able to do with the product of its Higgins Lake nursery as it is equipped today. These causes have been, first, lack of money, and, second, lack of men in some cases even when they had money for wages and to buy tools and equipment.

The program calls for opening two new forests each year. That has not been done. None were opened during the war period, and but one since the war ended. There has been labor available, in some districts where forests might have been opened, but not enough money for the purpose. The $55,000 a year undoubtedly is not enough to carry

—35—

out even the 2,000-acre planting plan of the past, considering rises in costs. It certainly is not enough to carry out the 4,500-acre planting industry.

Why exactly 4,500 acres, with some concrete facts in relation to decided on as the real requirement of Michigan's state-owned forest costs and returns will be the leading topic of the next article.

ARTICLE VIII.

In what has recently been written in these articles on the reclamation of Michigan bankrupt lands by means of a plan to restore the forests that once grew on them, the word "rotation" has been several times used, and probably not clearly understood by some readers.

Rotation of crop, in the case of a forest crop, means substantially that while two-year-old seedling trees are being taken out of the nursery and planted on the barren lands or in open spaces in the woods, earlier plantings have been growing toward maturity, each year's planted area being a 12-month step toward the goal. In the future years, when the state forester and his men shall begin harvesting Michigan's first timber crop, others of his men will be setting out on other lands "trees" that would make you laugh to look at, if you were wholly uninformed and out of sympathy with the work. These seedlings two years old are about as high out of the ground as your shoetop, and it is not till you fall to admiring a sturdy young tree shoulder high in the field and have been told that it has been there, say, seven years, that you begin to realize what forestry and forest cropping means.

BASIS OF PLAN.

Cutting off the matured crop at the end of the row and setting out spindling plants at the nursery end means rotating the crop. A simpler rotation than rotation of an agricultural crop, where one kind of crop is made to follow another, year by year—done in agriculture for the land's sake, principally.

"Of course we wouldn't want to cut off the whole crop of trees at one time, if we could," said Marcus Schaaf, state forester. "It takes too long to grow a crop. Constant supply of forest products is what is aimed at."

This is the basic reason for the 4,500-acre planting plan of the Michigan Public Domain Commission. More particularly, the 4,500-acre area is the allotment of total acreage in view for annual planting on the whole enormous state plantation, that the whole plantation may develop each year its proper area of matured crop. No need to inquire just how the state forester and the others arrived at this figure—one can afford to accept something from the paid experts without mangling his brain trying to master the intricacies of the science.

THE DOLLARS INVOLVED.

Now, as to the dollars involved, in outlay and return.

It has been stated, earlier, in perfect confidence, that the $55,000 the commission is getting cannot be expected to finance the 2,000-acre planting plan of the makeshift present. This is what the state forester tells the commission will be the necessary investment for the 4,500-acre plan for a period of years reaching out to maturity of the first planted area, his figures being based on the costs as they were in 1916:

There will have to be an annual expenditure of $150,000 for the first 30 years; for the second 30 years an annual outlay of $217,500.

The total investment during the 60 years would be $13,365,000.

The receipts at the end of the 60-year period, based on 1916 timber values, now vastly increased and bound to increase still more, would be $13,458,000.

INVESTMENT'S RETURN.

It is not to be assumed from these figures, however, that the forests would not do more than merely gain a relatively small profit for the state in all these years. Revenues would not wait on maturity of a crop. Long before the race between outlay and actual money return is won by the forests, the forests would become in fact self-supporting, and independent of legislative appropriations.

Therefore, it is not to be understood that "outlay" and "expenditure" of $150,000 a year for the first 30 years, and $217,500 during the next 30 years means state appropriations. It means that the forest industry which the state would capitalize out of its pocket would begin to put its money back into the business—when? Well, scrutiny of the elaborate figures of the forester seems to show that they would in about 30 years. The date has to be guessed at, for yields and prices have to be guessed at—yields easier to guess than prices. Considering that famine in forest products impends—in lumber and pulp wood especially—it doesn't wrench one's sense of probabilities to drag the self-supporting date for a properly conducted forest forward by several years.

INCREASE OF RECEIPTS.

At the beginning of the second period of rotation, when the first crop would be cut, says the forester, the receipts of that year would be several times the legislative appropriation, and that would continue to be the case, indefinitely. Then the forests would be turning into the state's general fund a net annual revenue much in excess of a-ual outlay.

And all this, as the forester says and repeats, and wisely, is set forth as a business proposition, pure and simple—board feet and cords again, with no allowance for reclamations of land too poor to pay even its taxes, no allowance for protection of wild life and making a desolate country attractive, and no allowance for gain in community values, towns revivified and people furnished with work and business.

The amateur inquirer, getting a sense of these values, naturally, before he gets a sense of the value of a tree, sometimes thinks the forester is standing in his own light by sticking so close to his business text. Every man to his trade, however; and it is clearly up to the man in the street to get, first, the immediate business argument, since it is a matter of investing his money in the project. When he has gotten that, it is an open question whether the returns in other things than money from timber are not business also. Certainly anything that enters into the labor of making a bankrupt empire first self-supporting and then remunerative appears to be a business proposition.

DUTY OF COMMISSION.

One plain duty of the Michigan Public Domain Commission is to take out of its shelved reports the 24-page study of State Forester Schaaf with all the elaborate tables, explaining the business aspect of the commission's work, and publish it as a pamphlet for Michigan citizens of business instinct to read—that is, if the commission knows where it can get the money to do it.

Turn now from the cost of tree-planting and the value of trees grown to a rapid view of the process of planting and taking care of plantations.

The state's plantations are on the cut-over pine lands. The pine was the prevailing occupant of the territory. Much hardwood there was, of course, taking the whole 650,000 acres of Public Domain Commission territory into view. Conifers, the "evergreens," grew on the poorer lands, however, and it is the poor lands that are being reclaimed by the commission.

This cuts down the number of species of trees dealt with, not only to the cone-bearing trees but it cuts down the conifers to four species. They are three natives and one foreigner. White Pine, Norway (red) Pine and Jack Pine grew on these worst devastated lands, and the White and Norway were the especial fruit of the devastating lumberman's ax.

FIRES GET PINE.

They grew on the uplands of sand or sand permeated with clay. In the lowlands grew many other varieties, also lumbered off, but not so cleanly in the early days as the big trees of the plains and hills.

Aiming first to restock the worst denuded lands, the state forester deals, then, with the native White Pine, Norway and Jack Pine. Fires and later lumbermen have been getting the Jack Pine which the earlier lumbermen scorned.

These three and one other are being planted. The other is the Scotch Pine. It nowhere grows native in this country—it is unknown to the lumber dealer. It is of the general nature of our native Jack Pine, but grows somewhat bulkier. There doesn't seem to be much choice between them, as to timber quality—both are inferior to White and Norway, prone to 'limbage," and consequently full of knots when sliced by the saw. Both can, and now do, enter into the making of pulp as a sort of adulterant of the essential Spruce, and both can be reckoned on for lath, box boards and the like.

PROTECT SWAMP TREES.

The value of the Scotch, like the Jack Pine is that it will grow on the poorest land. That makes it and the Jack Pine the foremost friend of man—of the men who have the job of reclaiming the worst of Michigan land.

White Pine is planted on the best lands, where White Pine originally grew; Norway with it, and also down on to the second best lands; and Jack and Scotch Pine on the thinnest lands. That is the general rule.

No Spruce to speak of, for that must grow on better lands than the White Pine requires. No hardwood, for essentially the same reason. Lowland and swamp trees are merely being protected and helped along by judicious thinning—reclamation in these cases waits on reclamation of the more barren areas.

It will be seen that the reclamation plan of the state's forestry department is modest, while it is nevertheless gigantic. The amount that needs to be done to put North Michigan back on a timber bearing basis on anything approaching the old-time scale is staggering to contemplate.

NEED GROWS DAILY.

"But," the reclamationists rightly argue, "the size of the job is no argument against beginning the work. Certainly not when the necessities of the case can be seen to be daily increasing, as well as the magnitude of the work of catching up. We can't begin sooner than now, and we can speed up according to our abilities as we go along."

"According to our abilities" means according to the amount of money the people who own the devastated land, the Michigan taxpayer, is willing to invest in the job to get it going and keep it going until the crop begins to return money that will make investment on capital account no longer necessary.

One hundred and fifty thousand dollars a year put into the job would mean for the average taxpayer about the price of one cheap cigar each year. The trouble the reclamationists appear to be in is to make the average citizens see the advantage of denying himself that one cigar a year. The trouble with the reclamationist is that he hasn't taken the public by the ear and made him listen.

The public will have an ear more sensitive to the argument when it knows more about the job and what progress is being made by the State to accomplish it, so furnishing an example for other land owners to follow. This leads back to operations on the state forest reserves, where tree-planting is but one of the two most important phases of the work. And this leads to the subjects of fire lines, fire towers, telephone system in the forests and similar matters. They will be discussed in the next article.

ARTICLE IX

A long, narrow road, a mere trail, rises in a sinuous line from the Jack Pine plain, in the Higgins Lake State Forest Reserve, to the top of a hill whereon looms against the sky the spidery tracery of a watch tower.

Sixty feet above the hilltop and far above the tops of trees on the hill slopes and in the valleys, on the square platform atop the tower, a youth in a vivid red sweater was lounging on the rail and casting his eyes around the horizon. This was on a Sunday afternoon a few weeks ago.

The season was far enough advanced to have brought on the early fire period in the forests. Spring is the worst time of the year; for then the green growth has not started and on the ground lies dead and dry as tinder the leaf fall of the year just past. Michigan's most expensive forest fires have occurred in May. It is true that the fires one hears most about often have raged in summer and fall. They were the spectacular fires occurring where tourists go and where newspaper correspondents have an eye trained for news. The fires that cost Michigan the most money have burned without publicity.

The youth in the red sweater knew all about this, as does every watchman, ranger and day laborer on the Michigan forest reserves. He was watching fires burn at this moment, but still he lounged, impassive.

There was smoke all around the horizon to the southwest and the wind was coming from that direction. It was a breeze that barely stirred one's coat tails, down on the ground, but aloft it was whistling through the wire netting of the watch tower guard rail. It was bringing up from the windward areas beyond the confines of the forest reservation a thin pall of smoke. Higgins Lake, two miles behind the watchman, but looking very near from the height of the hill, was dimly obscured.

GUARDED STATE PROPERTY.

The watchman worried not about the fires beyond the state forest limits, only watched to see if he could trace progression dangerously near to state property. So the afternoon hours drifted along. Suddenly from the foot of the tower the red sweater was seen coming down one steel leg of the structure, where loops of iron rod give a foot and hand hold. He went into a booth on the ground inside the tower, a shanty like the ones housing the telephones along an interurban railway line. He got headquarters on the phone and reported smoke inside the reservation. He gave an approximate location, using a jargon that sounded like a surveyor's statement.

What next happened could not be seen by the visitor, even by climbing up the tower, for it went on beneath the screen of intervening forests. This, however, was what was happening:

An automobile loaded with men and tools was putting out from headquarters several miles away and tearing through the sand roads toward the smudge which the watchman had reported. After going two or three miles over the twisting trails it struck into a straight strip of clearing that looked like a road but was not—a road only for forest fire fighters going at top speed to a fire. This was a fire line.

Sixteen feet wide, with a plowed and harrowed strip 10½ feet wide through the center of them, these fire lines stretch for many miles through the state forest, criss-crossing in geometrical precision. They are run on section, quarter-section and eighth-of-a-section lines.

It is told of a Russian Czar that, asked what route he would be pleased to have the then projected railway from St. Petersburg to Moscow follow, he laid a ruler on the map between the two cities, drew a line along the ruler and said: "Put it there."

TRACTOR DOES THE WORK.

That is how the state forester runs his fire lines. Over hill and down dale they go, skipping the swamps, never rounding them. On the Higgins Lake and nearby reserves a huge caterpillar tractor does the work, tearing out small trees and stumps, plowing the middle strip and keeping it harrowed. Elsewhere the work is done by horse-drawn equipment.

The automobile with the men and tools came upon the tiny fire in the grass near a point where a fire line crossed a highway. Perhaps somebody going past in an automobile had emptied a pipe or thrown out a cigar butt as he jogged past this spot. From the fire line the "smoke chasers" brought shovelsful of sand and smothered out the fire. It had gotten into the base of a dry old stump. They filled the crevices of the stump with fine sand; and the fire, out, had to stay out.

That is the forest fire fighter's material for fighting—dirt. That is the explanation of the 16-foot fire lines and the 10½-foot plowed strip along their centers.

When the forest fire fighter has to plunge into an unbroken wilderness of brush to cope with an incipient blaze by blanketing it out or by starting controllable backfires to starve it out, he works under a terrific handicap. By the time he gets ground broken and earth available the small blaze may have gotten beyond control. When there is a plowed fire line near he can at once get busy on the main job.

Some people of eminent position still carry the notion that fire lines are run with the idea that they stop the spread of fires by interposing an 'area from which combustible material has been removed. They do stop grass fires, but woods fires leap a 16-foot barrier with awesome ease.

The theory of the fire line is that it serves as a ready-made base of operations for the fire fighter—and the theory works out, as one can see for himself by looking at burnt-over tracts. Only a few weeks ago a 10-acre fire that started in one of the oldest plantations on the Higgins Lake Reserve burned up. to a fire line for a long stretch along the line, and there the ground was black and tree trunks charred. Sixteen feet away, on the other side of the line, stretched the forest without a trace of having been scorched.

ONLY ONE FOREST EQUIPPED.

A complete fire line system for the state's forests, in the plans of the Public Domain Commission, comprehends a line along the boundaries of every 40-acre tract within the reserve. But one forest has been thus completely equipped to date, but it is the only forest reserve in the United States that is. This is the Fyfe Lake Reserve of 7,182 acres area, 1,202 acres planted. The fire line mileage criss-crossing this forest totals 105 miles.

It costs from $100 to $150 a mile to run fire lines in the state's forests. It would cost about the same were it conceivable to run fire lines through the vast areas of fire country outside the reserves. The total would run into many millions, even were the section lines only followed. Nobody thinks of such a thing. Slash disposal and running of fire lines "to break up the most dangerous areas of slash," as Filibert Roth has put it, is the most in contemplation. When forests actually are set on the barrens, in the years to come, they doubtless will be protected by section and quarter-section lines.

The regulation forest fire fighting organization contemplates watchmen, patrolmen and smoke chasers. Watchmen in towers or stationed on hilltops spot smoke clouds and report. Patrolmen go about looking for fires, educating people on fire prevention and enforcing the fire laws. Smoke chasers go after the fires and put them out, calling in help when needed. The tools of the fire fighters are watch towers, telephone lines, grubhooks and shovels, and fire lines.

There is at least one watch-tower in each of the opened state forests, in three of them two towers each. These last are Houghton Lake, Lake Superior and Presque Isle. Phone lines from each communicate with the custodian's office in that particular forest, and thence to the outer world. It costs $100 a mile to put up these telephone equipments, where poles have to be erected. In some of the forests the lines hook up with other systems—as on Lake Superior Reserve, where there are arrangements with the United States Life-Saving Station on the Lake Superior shore within the limits of the state reservation.

STATE HAS DIFFICULTIES.

How much of the system in practice on the state reservations is applicable for the protection of natural growth and the propagation of replaced growth on the millions of state-owned and private-owned outside the reserves, the reader can easily figure out for himself, with one or two hints to guide his calculations. Matters of legality came into the reckoning. The status of state-owned and private-owned lands, in respect to protection costs, naturally differ. So does the fire line question, for it is one thing for the state to go out for a day's work on its own land, ripping things up, and quite another thing when the ripping is to be done on private land.

The state has its self-imposed handicaps. The Public Domain Commission has to get money from the Legislature to carry out a comprehensive, forward-looking scheme; but it is easy to 'perceive, on examination, that existing laws put upon private persons some handicaps in the way of restoration of barren acres to wealth production that the state has not set up in its own pathway.

One of these is the Timber Tax Law. This matter is important when the effort to get private interests into this great enterprise of restoring the bankrupt acres to wealth production is in mind. It will be given first consideration in the following articles, which will then point out a plan at this moment running through the minds of many people, whereby, if it desired to do so, the state could take the most threatening and neglected of privately-owned lands into its own hands and incorporate them in the development area it has laid out for its own activities.

ARTICLE X.

Restoration to Michigan's 10,000,000 bankrupt and near-bankrupt acres of cut-over pine lands of a permanent forest industry that will make these lands once more productive of wealth, rebuild decaying North Michigan towns and furnish auxiliary support for agricultural industry in a region where markets are scattered wide and labor too often can not find the winter employment with which to eke out the scanty livelihood which pioneer farms in the sand country afford— all this is involved as a prospect in the activities reflected in the beginnings that are being made by the Public Domain Commission on the state's reserved forest lands.

Private owners of large tracts have begun to show interest in the scheme, but they have not gone very far. Nothing is known in Michigan comparable to the organized activities of one of the big paper-making corporations over in Quebec, on the St. Maurice River. There a combination of pulp mill interests that controls 15,000 square miles of timber land has a nursery for production of white spruce seedlings. Planting is going on, it is claimed, at the rate of more than 1,000,000 trees a year. Michigan's forestry department plants about 3,000,000 each year. The only Michigan corporation heard of as interested in this work on a comparable scale is a mining corporation in the Upper Peninsula which has been lately inquiring for prices on seedling trees in million lots.

SEEDLINGS AT COSTS.

"We can furnish 1,000,000 seedlings a year," said A. K. Chittenden, head of the forestry department of the Michigan Agricultural College. "We gave this company a quotation a year ago, but have heard nothing from them since."

M. A. C., like the state nursery at Higgins Lake, sells seedlings at cost. The college nursery of 29 acres supplies seedlings for sand land owned by the college up north and does a big businesss in promoting propagation of trees in farmers' wood lots and along public highways all over the state.

"The trouble, when you come to consider private interests in relation to the problem of re-clothing idle lands with forests," said Orlando F. Barnes, of the State Tax Commission, "is that timber yields no income to the owner until separated from the soil. The owners are under constant pressure to cut and market. There is a constantly increasing tax burden, with no similar annual income to meet it. Michigan forests are taxed as real estate. The increase in value of the trees is taxed each year, while the harvest waits. It must wait for many years.

TIMBER HARVEST WAITS.

"The premise is a false one. The supposition is that the forest has but one year's life, like the ordinary crop of a farmer. Farm crops aren't even taxed, direct. The land is taxed according to its crop raising capabilities as proved by the yields from year to year. We don't tax the corn and the wheat as it stands on the land, but we do tax the timber. While the harvest with which to pay the tax bills waits, from 30 to 75 years as the case may be, the owner must pay from year to year. He must get the money from some other source. Not only that, but interest on the outlay compounds at a staggering rate.

"Land and timber should be exempted from the annual ad valorem property tax, and there should be substituted for it a percentage tax payable whenever any part of the timber crop is harvested. This should be modified by an annual land tax at a fixed rate upon the land valued as stump land, along with a yield tax when the timber is cut. There must be a fixed land tax collected annually, for the counties in which these lands are located must have their revenue."

CAN'T AFFORD TREE-PLANTING.

This explains, in outline, statements which have been made to the inquirer among owners of large, unused areas in the bankrupt land area. The question was asked: "Why don't you re-establish the forests on these lands?"

The answer always is: "Because we can't afford to do it when the state taxes us to death"—a statement never made clear by them, but now explained by the state tax commissioner.

Among residents of the North country there is to this day a fixed antagonism to any scheme that contemplates easement of the tax burden on these lands. The counties need the money. The fact that 3,00 acres a month revert to the state for non-payment of taxes doesn't tend to loosen the local grip. There is, however, now evident and becoming yearly more evident, a conviction that fire damage wrought by conflagrations starting in slash lands can not be brought into bounds without some action that will give the state and its fire-fighting and tree-planting organizations more direct control over private lands than they now have. It is useless to expect owners of charred and devastated sand plains to do anything effective. That is the conviction among thinking men in the northern counties.

GETTING TOGETHER.

A proposal has bobbed up in agricultural circles. It is there, indeed, that something might have been expected to occur. The fact that ag-

—43—

riculturists have a plan for control of the forest fire menace at the same time serves to point out an important fact—which is that interests which hitherto have been at variance are at last coming together. Farmers are beginning to get in on the foresters' problem, in a helpful way, at least hereabouts, that is, in the area of the Lake States.

The Northwest Michigan Development Bureau, with headquarters at Traverse City, in the general location where have occurred the worst of the Lower Peninsula forest fires of recent date, adopted at one of its meetings not long ago a set of resolutions calling for state control and administration of the worst of the slash lands.

"Thousands of acres of cut-over land lying idle in Michigan are a menace to surrounding lands. They are a breeding place for grasshoppers and are fire traps," say these agriculturists; and when they speak of fire they have the full accord of Upper Peninsula men on grazing lands, whose flocks and herds have been driven many miles at times by fire, often perishing.

PASTURAGE SUGGESTED.

Say the Northwestern Michigan agriculturists: "It is possible to handle these lands in such a manner that all lands suitable to. reforestation could be planted and cared for; and all lands suitable for pasturage could be used for that purpose.

"Cut-over pine lands not owned by the state could be condemned, a just value placed by a competent board of appraisers and the owners reimbursed. This should be done only when a majority of the freeholders of a township or a county request it. The township or county requesting such action by the state could agree to keep the fire lines open, the initial cost to be borne by the state. The township or county could also agree to maintain a fire warden.

The shrewd policy dictating this proposal may not at first appear to the general reader. Here is a proposition, not for the state to step on to private lands, perhaps at the behest of a state forestry department which wants acres allotted to it for free planting, but for communities themselves to put the first stigma of non-agricultural availability and existing menace upon private property—the state to accede to the proposition only on proofs arising among the people who know the lands as neighbors and naturally would be interested in seeing the land exploited for agriculture, if there were any hope of that outcome.

PRIVILEGE TO COUNTY.

"In order to furnish an incentive for a township or county to make such a request (for condemnation)," the north country men continue, "the state could agree to reforest such land as would be suitable for reforestation and give the township or county the privilege of pasturing cattle on the land. This would be a great boon for the live stock industry, as the live stock men would be reasonably sure that fires would not destroy their pastures in the middle of the season."

North Michigan live stock men are taking a leaf from the book of the western herdsmen. First fighting forest conservation, these latter finally became reconciled to grazing fees on Federal forest lands, finally finding, by all accounts, that the forest conservation "cranks" were actually working to the stockmen's advantage. Grazing fees pay a large part of the forest activities on Government lands in the West.

"Making the township or county a co-operator would insure a greater measure of success than would be possible in a state undertaking," conclude the North Michigan men. "It might be made compulsory for a township or county having a certain percentage of its land either wild or cut-over to take such action."

As a mere unofficial, voluntary proposal for state legislation calculating to cope with phases of an enormous problem, here is a suggestion concrete and plausible enough for anybody, on the face of it. It seems to make suggestively practicable Prof. Roth's demand that "the worst and most threatening area of slash lands be broken up" as a fire protection measure.

"CUT SLASH TO GROUND."

The state's laws regarding slash disposal need to be worked out to more definite and practical conclusions than now provided for. This needs to be done if farmers and ranchmen are to be properly protected and if the state's forests are to be protected without disproportionate cost. Two years ago fires coming up out of the slash lands burned over farms and waste places in the area of Higgins Laks reserve until they had come up to a line 22 miles long, which is within two miles of the total of the line bounding the forest. Some of them got into the forest and were there controlled.

"Slash shouldn't be disposed of by being burned," said State Forester Schaaf. "I don't believe in destroying anything. Slash should be cut down to the ground. There it is far less liable to spread fire, and soon it rots away, going back into the soil which needs it."

What has been said earlier in these articles on matters of required appropriations for work will have to suffice, as suggesting legislation. This includes what Mr. Lovejoy has so clearly expounded regarding the necessities of a land survey, to go hand in hand with reclamation activities and to give direction to replanting effort and the expenditure of funds for fire protection.

A large subject remains—the explanation of what reforestation of these barren lands will mean to industrial Michigan and the life of dwellers in North Michigan towns, as also the lives of people who only occasionally visit the north country. Those things will have to await treatment at another time.